The GREAT APOSTASY

Considered in the Light of Scriptural and Secular History

BY

JAMES E. TALMAGE

D. Sc. D., Ph. D., F. R. S. E.

Published by
DESERET BOOK COMPANY
Salt Lake City, Utah
1977

ISBN No. 0-87747-384-6

Lithographed by

DESERET PRESS

in the United States of America

PREFACE

The Church of Jesus Christ of Latter-day Saints proclaims the restoration of the Gospel, and the re-establishment of the Church as of old, in this, the Dispensation of the Fulness of Times. Such restoration and re-establishment, with the modern bestowal of the Holy Priesthood, would be unnecessary and indeed impossible had the Church of Christ continued among men with unbroken succession of Priesthood and power, since the "meridian of time."

The restored Church affirms that a general apostasy developed during and after the apostolic period, and that the primitive Church lost its power, authority, and graces as a divine institution, and degenerated into an earthly organization only. The significance and importance of the great apostasy, as a condition precedent to the re-establishment of the Church in modern times, is obvious. If the alleged apostasy of the primitive Church was not a reality, The Church of Jesus Christ of Latter-day Saints is not the divine institution its name proclaims.

The evidence of the decline and final extinction of the primitive Church among men is found in scriptural record, and in secular history. In the following pages the author has undertaken to present a summary of the most important of these evidences. In so doing he has drawn liberally from many sources of information, with due acknowledgment of all citations. The little work has been written in the hope that it may prove of service to our missionary elders in the field, to classes and quorum organizations engaged in the study of theological subjects at home, and to earnest investigators of the teachings and claims of the restored Church of Jesus Christ.

JAMES E. TALMAGE.

SALT LAKE CITY, UTAH.

November 1, 1909.

CONTENTS

CONTENTS

CHAPTER IX.

INTERNAL CAUSES.—CONTINUED.

CHAPTER X.

RESULTS OF THE APOSTASY.—ITS SEQUEL.

The

GREAT APOSTASY

CHAPTER I.

INTRODUCTION: THE ESTABLISHMENT OF THE CHURCH OF CHRIST.

1. A belief common to all sects and churches professing Christianity is that Jesus Christ, the Savior and Redeemer of the human race, established His Church upon the earth, by personal ministration in the meridian of time. Ecclesiastical history, as distinguished from secular history, deals with the experiences of the Church from the time of its establishment. The conditions under which the Church was founded first claim our attention.

2. At the beginning of the Christian era, the Jews, in common with most other nations, were subjects of the Roman empire.[a] They were allowed a considerable degree of liberty in maintaining their religious observances and national customs generally, but their status was far from that of a free and independent people.

3. The period was one of comparative peace—a time marked by fewer wars and less dissension than the empire had known for many years. These conditions were favorable for the mission of the Christ, and for the founding of His Church on earth.

---

[a]See Note 1, end of chapter.

4. The religious systems extant at the time of Christ's earthly ministry may be classified in a general way as Jewish and Pagan, with a minor system—the Samaritan—which was essentially a mixture of the other two. The children of Israel alone proclaimed the existence of the true and living God; they alone looked forward to the advent of the Messiah, whom mistakenly they awaited as a prospective conqueror coming to crush the enemies of their nation. All other nations, tongues, and peoples, bowed to pagan deities, and their worship comprised nought but the sensual rites of heathen idolatry. Paganism[b] was a religion of form and ceremony, based on polytheism—a belief in the existence of a multitude of gods, which deities were subject to all the vices and passions of humanity, while distinguished by immunity from death. Morality and virtue were unknown as elements of heathen service; and the dominant idea in pagan worship was that of propitiating the gods, in the hope of averting their anger and purchasing their favor.

5. The Israelites, or Jews as they were collectively known, thus stood apart among the nations as proud possessors of superior knowledge, with a lineage and a literature, with a priestly organization and a system of laws, that separated and distinguished them as a people at once peculiar and exclusive. While the Jews regarded their idolatrous neighbors with abhorrence and contempt, they in turn were treated with derision as fanatics and inferiors.

6. But the Jews, while thus distinguished as a people from the rest of the world, were by no means a united people; on the contrary they were divided among themselves

---

[b]See Note 2, end of chapter.

on matters of religious profession and practice. In the first place, there was a deadly enmity between the Jews proper and the Samaritans. These latter were a mixed people inhabiting a distinct province mostly between Judea and Galilee, largely made up of Assyrian colonists who had intermarried with the Jews. While affirming their belief in the Jehovah of the Old Testament, they practiced many rites belonging to the paganism they claimed to have forsaken, and were regarded by the Jews proper as unorthodox and reprobate.

7. Then the Jews themselves were divided into many contending sects and parties, among which the principal were the Pharisees and the Sadducees; and beside these we read of Essenes, Galileans, Herodians, etc.

8. The Jews were living under the Law of Moses, the outward observance of which was enforced by priestly rule, while the spirit of the law was very generally ignored by priest and people alike. That the Mosaic law was given as a preparation for something greater was afterward affirmed by Paul, in his epistle to the saints at Galatia: "Wherefore the law was our schoolmaster to bring us unto Christ."[c] And the fact that a higher law was to supersede the lower is abundantly shown in the Savior's own teachings: "Ye have heard that it was said by them of old time, Thou shalt not kill; and whosoever shall kill shall be in danger of the judgment: But I say unto you that whosoever is angry with his brother without a cause shall be in danger of the judgment: * * * Ye have heard that it was said by them of old time, Thou shalt not commit adultery: But I say unto you that whosoever looketh on a woman to lust after her hath committed adultery with her already in his heart.

---

[c]Galatians 3:24.

* * * Again, ye have heard that it hath been said by them of old time, Thou shalt not forswear thyself but shalt perform unto the Lord thine oaths: But I say unto you, Swear not at all. * * * Ye have heard that it hath been said, An eye for an eye and a tooth for a tooth: But I say unto you that ye resist not evil. * * * Ye have heard that it hath been said, Thou shalt love thy neighbor and hate thine enemy. But I say unto you, Love your enemies, bless them that curse you, do good to them that hate you, and pray for them which despitefully use you and persecute you."[d]

9. These teachings, based on love, so different from the spirit of retaliation to which they had been accustomed under the law, caused great surprise among the people; yet in affirmation of the fact that the law was not to be ignored, and could only be superseded by its fulfilment, the Master said: "Think not that I am come to destroy the law, or the prophets: I am not come to destroy but to fulfil. For verily I say unto you, Till heaven and earth pass, one jot or one tittle shall in no wise pass from the law till all be fulfilled."[e]

10. It is very evident that the Master had come with a greater doctrine than was then known, and that the teachings of the day were insufficient: "For I say unto you that except your righteousness shall exceed the righteousness of the scribes and Pharisees, ye shall in no case enter into the kingdom of heaven."[f]

11. Jesus Himself was strict in complying with all rightful requirements under the law; but He refused to recognize

[d]Matthew 5:21-44; read the entire chapter.
[e]Matt. 5: 17, 18.
[f]Verse 20.

an observance of the letter alone, however rigidly required, as a substitute for compliance with the spirit of the Mosaic injunction.

12. The excellent teachings and precepts of true morality inculcated by the Christ prepared the minds of those who believed His words for the introduction of the gospel in its purity, and for the establishment of the Church of Christ as an earthly organization.

13. From among the disciples who followed Him, some of whom had been honored by preliminary calls, He chose twelve men, whom He ordained to the apostleship:—"And he ordained twelve, that they should be with him and that he might send them forth to preach."[g] Again: "And when it was day, he called unto him his disciples: and of them he chose twelve whom also he named apostles."[h] The twelve special witnesses of Him and His work were sent out to preach in the several cities of the Jews. On this, their first mission, they were instructed to confine their ministrations to the house of Israel, and the burden of their message was "The kingdom of heaven is at hand."[i] They were told to use the power with which they had been invested by ordination, in preaching, in healing the sick, in raising the dead even, and in subduing evil spirits; the Master's admonition was, "Freely ye have received, freely give." They were to travel without money or provisions, relying upon a higher power to supply their needs through the agency of those to whom they would offer the message of truth; and they were warned of the possible hardships awaiting them

[g]Mark 3: 14.
[h]Luke 6: 13; compare Matt. 10: 1, 2.
[i]Matt. 10: 7; study the entire chapter.

and of the persecution which sooner or later would surely befall them.

14. At a later date Christ called others to the work of the ministry, and sent them out in pairs to precede Him and prepare the people for His coming. Thus we read of "the seventy" who were instructed in terms almost identical with those of the apostolic commission.[j] That their investiture was one of authority and power and no mere form is shown by the success attending their administrations; for when they returned they reported triumphantly, "Lord, even the devils are subject unto us through thy name."[k]

15. The specific commission given unto the apostles at the time of their ordination was afterward emphasized. They were the subjects of the particularly solemn ordinance spoken of as the washing of feet, so necessary that in reply to Peter's objection the Lord said: "If I wash thee not thou hast no part with me."[l] And unto the eleven who had remained faithful, the Risen Lord delivered His parting instructions, immediately before the ascension: "Go ye into all the world and preach the gospel to every creature." After our Lord's departure the apostles entered upon the ministry with vigor: "And they went forth and preached everywhere, the Lord working with them, and confirming the word with signs following."[m]

16. These scriptures indicate the authority of the apostles to administer the affairs of the Church after the ascension of the Resurrected Messiah. That Peter, the senior member of the apostolic council, was given a position of

[j]Luke 10; compare with Matt. 10.
[k]Luke 10: 17.
[l]John 13: 4-9.
[m]Mark 16: 14-20; compare Matt. 28: 19, 20.

presidency, appears from the Savior's special admonition and charge on the shores of the Tiberian sea."

17. That the apostles realized that though the Master had gone He had left with them authority and command to build up the Church as an established organization, is abundantly proved by scripture. They first proceeded to fill the vacancy in the presiding council or "quorum" of twelve, a vacancy occasioned by the apostasy and death of Judas Iscariot; and the mode of procedure in this official act is instructive. The installation of a new apostle was not determined by the eleven alone; we read that the disciples (or members of the Church) were gathered together—about a hundred and twenty in number. To them Peter presented the matter requiring action, and emphasized the fact that the man to be chosen must be one who had personal knowledge and testimony of the Lord's ministry, and who was therefore qualified to speak as a special witness of the Christ, which qualification is the distinguishing feature of the apostleship. "Wherefore," said Peter, "of these men which have companied with us all the time that the Lord Jesus went in and out among us, beginning from the baptism of John, unto that same day that he was taken up from us, must one be ordained to be a witness with us of his resurrection."° We are further informed that two men were nominated, and that the divine power was invoked to show whether either, and if so, which, was the Lord's choice. Then the votes were cast "and the lot fell upon Matthias; and he was numbered with the eleven apostles."

18. It is evident that the apostles considered their council or quorum as definitely organized with a membership

---

*John 21: 15-17.
°Acts 1: 21, 22; read verses 15-26 inclusive.

limit of twelve; and that the work of the Church required
that the organization be made complete. Nevertheless, we
read of none others subsequently chosen to fill vacancies in
the council of twelve. Paul, who previous to his conversion
was known as Saul of Tarsus, received a special manifestation, in which he heard the voice of the Risen Lord declaring "I am Jesus whom thou persecutest,"[p] and thereby he
became a special witness of the Lord Jesus, and as such was
in truth an apostle, though we have no definite scriptural
record that he was ever made a member of the council of
twelve. As showing the importance of ordination to office
under the hands of duly constituted authorities, we have the
instance of Paul's ordination. Though he had conversed
with the Resurrected Jesus, though he had been the subject
of a special manifestation of divine power in the restoration
of his sight, he had nevertheless to be baptized; and later
he was commissioned for the work of the ministry by the
authoritative imposition of hands.[q]

19.   Another instance of official action in choosing and
setting apart men to special office in the Church arose soon
after the ordination of Matthias. It appears that one feature
of the Church organization in early apostolic days was a
common ownership of material things, distribution being
made according to need. As the members increased, it was
found impracticable for the apostles to devote the necessary attention and time to these temporal matters, so they
called upon the members to select seven men of honest report, whom the apostles would appoint to take special
charge of these affairs. These men were set apart by prayer
and by the laying on of hands.[r] The instance is instructive

[p]Acts 9: 5; read verses 1-22.
[q]Acts 13: 1-3.

as showing that the apostles realized their possession of authority to direct in the affairs of the Church, and that they observed with strict fidelity the principle of common consent in the administration of their high office. They exercised their priestly powers in the spirit of love, and with due regard to the rights of the people over whom they were placed to preside.

20.　Under the administration of the apostles, and others who labored by their direction in positions of lesser authority, the Church grew in numbers and influence.[s] For ten or twelve years after the ascension of Christ, Jerusalem remained the headquarters of the Church, but branches or, as designated in the scriptural record, separate "churches," were established in the outlying provinces. As such branches were organized, bishops, deacons, and other officers were chosen, and doubtless ordained by authority, to minister in local affairs.[t]

21.　That the commission of the Lord Jesus to the apostles, instructing them to preach the gospel widely, was executed with promptness and zeal, is evident from the rapid growth of the Church in the early apostolic times.[u] Paul, writing about A. D. 64 — approximately thirty years after the ascension — declares that the gospel had already been carried to every nation — "preached to every creature under heaven,"[v] by which expression the apostle doubtless means that the gospel message had been so generally proclaimed, that all who would might learn of it.

---

[r] Acts 6: 1-7.
[s] See Note 3, end of chapter.
[t] See Philip. 1: 1; compare I Tim. 3: 1, 2, 8, 10.
[u] Acts 6: 7; 12: 24; 19: 20.
[v] Col. 1: 23; compare verse 6.

22.   Details as to the organization of the Church in apostolic days are not given with great fulness. As already shown, the presiding authority was vested in the twelve apostles; and furthermore, the special calling of the seventies has received attention; but beside these there were evangelists, pastors, and teachers,[w] and in addition, high priests,[x] elders,[y] bishops,[z] etc. The purpose of these several offices is explained by Paul to be:—"For the perfecting of the saints, for the work of the ministry, for the edifying of the body of Christ."[a] The Church with its graded offices and its spiritual gifts has been aptly compared to a perfect body with its separate organs and its individual members, each necessary to the welfare of the whole, yet none independent of the rest. As in the human organism so in the Church of Christ, no one with propriety can say to another, "I have no need of thee."[b]

THE CHURCH OF CHRIST ON THE WESTERN HEMISPHERE.

23.   We have seen, on the evidence of the Jewish scriptures, how the Church was established and made strong in Asia and Europe in and immediately following the meridian of time. The scriptures cited are such as appeal to all earnest Christians; the authority is that of the New Testament. We have now to consider the establishment of the Church amongst those who constituted another division of

---

[w]Eph. 4: 11.
[x]Heb. 5: 1-5.
[y]Acts 14: 23; 15: 6; I Peter 5: 1.
[z]I Tim. 3: 1; Titus 1: 7.
[a]Eph. 4: 12; read also verses 13-16.
[b]See I Cor. 12. See Note 4, end of chapter.

the house of Israel—a people inhabiting what is now known as the American continent.

24. For the benefit of those who are unfamiliar with the Nephite scriptures, published to the world as the Book of Mormon, a brief historical summary is here presented.[c] In the year 600 B. C., in the reign of King Zedekiah, a small colony was led from Jerusalem by an inspired prophet named Lehi. These people were brought by divine assistance to the shores of the Arabian Sea, where they constructed a vessel in which they crossed the great waters to the western coast of South America. They landed 590 B. C. The people were soon divided into two parties, led respectively by Nephi and Laman, sons of Lehi; and these factions grew into the opposing nations known in history as Nephites and Lamanites. The former developed while the latter retrograded in the arts of civilization. Nephite prophets predicted the earthly advent of the Messiah, and foretold His ministry, crucifixion, and resurrection.

25. The record states that the Messiah appeared in person among the Nephites on the western continent. This was subsequent to His ascension from the Mount of Olives. A foreshadowing of this great event was given by Christ in a declaration made while yet He lived on earth. Comparing Himself to the good shepherd who giveth his life for the sheep, He said: "And other sheep I have which are not of this fold; them also I must bring, and they shall hear my voice, and there shall be one fold and one shepherd."[d]

26. According to the Nephite record, certain predicted signs of the Savior's death had come to pass. Destructive

---

[c]See Note 5, end of chapter.
[d]John 10: 16; read verses 1-18 inclusive. Compare III Nephi 15: 21.

earthquakes and other dread convulsions of nature had taken place in the west, while the supreme tragedy was being enacted on Calvary. The people of the land Bountiful, comprising the northern portion of South America, were still marveling over the great convulsions that had so terrified them a few weeks earlier, and, on a certain occasion, were gathered together discussing the matter, when they heard a voice as from the heavens saying: "Behold my beloved Son, in whom I am well pleased, in whom I have glorified my name; hear ye him."[e] Looking up they beheld a man descending. He was clothed in a white robe, and as he reached the earth he said: "Behold, I am Jesus Christ, whom the prophets testified shall come into the world. * * * Arise and come forth unto me that ye may thrust your hands into my side, and also that ye may feel the prints of the nails in my hands and in my feet; that ye may know that I am the God of Israel, and the God of the whole earth, and have been slain for the sins of the world."[f]

27. Having thus declared Himself, Christ proceeded to instruct the people in the plan of the gospel as He had preached it, and in the constitution of the Church as He had established it in the east. He visited the Nephite people on subsequent occasions, taught them many of the precepts previously given to the Jews; emphasized the doctrine of baptism and other ordinances essential to salvation; instituted the sacrament in commemoration of His atoning death; chose and commissioned twelve apostles, on whom He conferred authority in the Church; explained the importance of designating the organization by its proper name —the Church of Christ; and announced the fulfilment of the

[e]III Nephi 11: 7; read the entire chapter.
[f]Verses 10, 14.

law of Moses and the fact that it was thenceforth superseded
by the gospel embodied within the Church as established by
Himself. In plan of organization, in doctrine and precept,
and in prescribed ordinances, the Church of Christ in the
west was the counter-part of the Church in Palestine.

———

28. Thus in the meridian of time the Church of God
was founded on both sides of the earth. In its pristine
simplicity and beauty is exhibited the majesty of a divine
institution. It is now our saddening duty to consider the decline of spiritual power within the Church, and the eventual
apostasy of the Church itself.

Notes.

1. CONDITIONS AT THE BEGINNING OF THE CHRISTIAN ERA. "At
the birth of Christ this amazing federation of the world into one
great monarchy had been finally achieved. Augustus, at Rome, was
the sole power to which all nations looked. * * * No prince, no
king, no potentate of any name could break the calm which such a
universal dominion secured. * * * It was in such a unique era
that Jesus Christ was born. The whole earth lay hushed in profound
peace. All lands lay freely open to the message of mercy and love
which He came to announce. Nor was the social and moral conditions of the world at large, at the birth of Christ, less fitting for His
advent than the political. The prize of universal power struggled for
through sixty years of plots and desolating civil wars, had been won
at last by Augustus. Sulla and Marius, Pompey and Caesar, had led
their legions against each other, alike in Italy and the provinces, and
had drenched the earth with blood. Augustus himself had reached
the throne only after thirteen years of war, which involved regions
wide apart. The world was exhausted by the prolonged agony of such
a strife; it sighed for repose." (Cunningham Geikie, "The Life and
Works of Christ;" New York, 1894; vol. I, p. 25.)

"The Roman empire, at the birth of Christ, was less agitated
by wars and turmoils than it had been for many years before. For

though I cannot assent to the opinion of those who, following the account of Orosius, maintain that the temple of Janus was then shut, and that wars and discords absolutely ceased throughout the world, yet it is certain that the period in which our Savior descended upon earth may be justly styled the 'pacific age,' if we compare it with the preceding times. And indeed the tranquility that then reigned was necessary to enable the ministers of Christ to execute with success their sublime commission to the human race." (Mosheim, "Ecclesiastical History," Cent. I, Part I; ch. 1: 4.)

2. PAGANISM AT THE BEGINNING OF THE CHRISTIAN ERA. "Every nation then had its respective gods, over which presided one more excellent than the rest; yet in such a manner that this supreme deity was himself controlled by the rigid empire of the facts, or what the philosophers called 'external necessity.' The gods of the east were different from those of the Gauls, the Germans, and the other northern nations. The Grecian divinities differed widely from those of the Egyptians, who deified plants, animals, and a great variety of the productions both of nature and art. Each people also had their own particular manner of worshiping and appeasing their respective deities, entirely different from the sacred rites of other countries. ° ° One thing, indeed, which at first sight appears very remarkable, is, that this variety of religions and of gods neither produced wars nor dissensions among the different nations, the Egyptians excepted. Nor is it perhaps necessary to except even them, since their wars undertaken for their gods cannot be looked upon with propriety as wholly of a religious nature. Each nation suffered its neighbors to follow their own method of worship, to adore their own gods, to enjoy their own rites and ceremonies, and discovered no sort of displeasure at their diversity of sentiments in religious matters. There is, however, little wonderful in this spirit of mutual toleration, when we consider that they all looked upon the world as one great empire, divided into various provinces, over every one of which a certain order of divinities presided; and that therefore none could behold with contempt the gods of other nations, or force strangers to pay homage to theirs. The Romans exercised this toleration in the amplest manner. For, though they would not allow any changes to be made in the religions that were publicly professed in the empire, nor any new form of worship to be openly introduced,

yet they granted to their citizens a full liberty of observing in private the sacred rites of other nations, and of honoring foreign deities (whose worship contained nothing inconsistent with the interests and laws of the republic) with feasts, temples, consecrated groves and such like testimonies of homage and respect." (Mosheim, "Eccl. Hist.," Cent. I, Part I: ch. 1: 7-8.)

3. RAPID GROWTH OF THE CHURCH. Eusebius, who wrote in the early part of the fourth century, speaking of the first decade after the Savior's ascension, says:

"Thus, then, under a celestial influence and co-operation, the doctrine of the Savior, like the rays of the sun, quickly irradiated the whole world. Presently, in accordance with divine prophecy, the sound of His inspired evangelists and apostles had gone throughout all the earth, and their words to the ends of the world. Throughout every city and village, like a replenished barn floor, churches were rapidly abounding and filled with members from every people. Those who, in consequence of the delusions that had descended to them from their ancestors, had been fettered by the ancient disease of idolatrous superstition, were now liberated by the power of Christ, through the teachings and miracles of His messengers." (Eusebius, "Ecclesiastical History," Book I, ch. 3.)

4. DIVINE INSTRUMENTALITY IN THE APOSTOLIC MINISTRY. "When we consider the rapid progress of Christianity among the Gentile nations, and the poor and feeble instruments by which this great and amazing event was immediately effected, we naturally have recourse to an omnipotent and invisible hand, as its true and proper cause. For, unless we suppose here a divine interposition, how was it possible that men, destitute of all human aid, without credit or riches, learning, or eloquence, could, in so short a time, persuade a considerable part of mankind to abandon the religion of their ancestors? How was it possible that an handful of apostles, who, as fishermen and publicans, must have been contemned by their own nation, and as Jews must have been odious to all others, could engage the learned and mighty, as well as the simple and those of low degree, to forsake their favorite prejudices, and to embrace a new religion which was an enemy to their corrupt passions? And,

indeed, there were undoubtedly marks of a celestial power per-
petually attending their ministry. There was in their very language,
an incredible energy, an amazing power of sending light into the
understanding, and conviction into the heart." (Mosheim, "Ecclesiastical History," Cent. I, Part I, ch. 4: 8.)

5. NEPHITES AND LAMANITES. The progenitors of the Nephite
nation "were led from Jerusalem, 600 B. C., by Lehi, a Jewish
prophet of the tribe of Manasseh. His immediate family, at the
time of their departure from Jerusalem, comprised his wife Sariah,
and their sons, Laman, Lemuel, Sam, and Nephi; at a later stage
of the history, daughters are mentioned, but whether any of these
were born before the family exodus we are not told. Besides his
own family, the colony of Lehi included Zoram, and Ishmael, the
latter an Israelite of the tribe of Ephraim. Ishmael, with his family,
joined Lehi in the wilderness; and his descendants were numbered
with the nations of whom we are speaking. The company journeyed
somewhat east of south, keeping near the borders of the Red Sea;
then, changing their course to the eastward, crossed the peninsula
of Arabia; and there, on the shores of the Arabian Sea, built and
provisioned a vessel in which they committed themselves to Divine
care upon the waters. Their voyage carried them eastward across
the Indian Ocean, then over the south Pacific Ocean to the western
coast of South America, whereon they landed (590 B. C.) • • • •
The people established themselves on what to them was the land
of promise; many children were born, and in the course of a few
generations a numerous posterity held possession of the land. After
the death of Lehi, a division occurred, some of the people accepting
as their leader, Nephi, who had been duly appointed to the prophetic
office; while the rest proclaimed Laman, the eldest of Lehi's sons, as
their chief. Henceforth the divided people were known as Nephites
and Lamanites respectively. At times they observed toward each other
fairly friendly relations; but generally they were opposed, the Lamanites manifesting implacable hatred and hostility toward their Nephite
kindred. The Nephites advanced in the arts of civilization, built
large cities and established prosperous commonwealths; yet they
often fell into transgression; and the Lord chastened them by making
their foes victorious. They spread northward, occupying the northern

part of South America; then, crossing the Isthmus, they extended their domain over the southern, central and eastern portions of what is now the United States of America. The Lamanites, while increasing in numbers, fell under the curse of darkness; they became dark in skin and benighted in spirit, forgot the God of their fathers, lived a wild and nomadic life, and degenerated into the fallen state in which the American Indians—their lineal descendants—were found by those who re-discovered the western continent in later times." (The Author, "Articles of Faith," Lect. 14: 7, 8.)

CHAPTER II.

1. In proceeding with our present inquiry we accept as demonstrated facts the establishment of the Church of Christ under the Savior's personal administration and the rapid growth of the Church in the early period of the apostolic ministry.

2. A question of the utmost importance is: Has the Church of Christ, thus authoritatively established, maintained an organized existence upon the earth from the apostolic age to the present? Other questions are suggested by the first. If the Church has continued as an earthly organization, where lies the proof or evidence of legitimate succession in priestly authority, and which among the multitude of contending sects or churches of the present day is the actual possessor of the holy priesthood originally committed to the Church by the Christ, its founder?

3. Again, have the spiritual gifts and graces by which the early Church was characterized and distinguished been manifest on earth through the centuries that have passed since the meridian of time; and if so, in which of the numerous churches of these modern times do we find such signs following the professed believers?[a]

4. We affirm that with the passing of the so-called apostolic age the Church gradually drifted into a condition of apostasy, whereby succession in the priesthood was broken; and that the Church, as an earthly organization operating

---

[a] See Mark 16: 17.

under divine direction and having authority to officiate in spiritual ordinances, ceased to exist.

5. If therefore the Church of Christ is to be found upon the earth today it must have been re-established by divine authority; and the holy priesthood must have been restored to the world from which it was lost by the apostasy of the Primitive Church.[b]

6. We affirm that the great apostasy was foretold by the Savior Himself while He lived as a Man among men, and by His inspired prophets both before and after the period of His earthly probation. And further, we affirm that a rational interpretation of history demonstrates the fact of this great and general apostasy.

7. Before we take up in detail the specific predictions referred to, and the evidence of their dread fulfilment, we may profitably devote brief attention to certain general considerations.

8. Respecting the foreknowledge of God, let it not be said that divine omniscience is of itself a determining cause whereby events are inevitably brought to pass. A mortal father who knows the weaknesses and frailties of his son may by reason of that knowledge sorrowfully predict the calamities and sufferings awaiting his wayward boy. He may foresee in that son's future a forfeiture of blessings that could have been won, loss of position, self-respect, reputation and honor; even the dark shadows of a felon's cell and the night of a drunkard's grave may appear in the saddening visions of that fond father's soul; yet, convinced by experience of the impossibility of bringing about that son's reform, he foresees the dread developments of the future, and he finds but sorrow and anguish in his knowledge.

---

[b]See Note 1, end of chapter.

Can it be said that the father's foreknowledge is a cause
of the son's sinful life? The son, perchance, has reached
his maturity; he is the master of his own destiny; a free
agent unto himself. The father is powerless to control by
force or to direct by arbitrary command; and, while he
would gladly make any effort or sacrifice to save his son
from the fate impending, he fears for what seems to be
an awful certainty. But surely that thoughtful, prayerful,
loving parent does not contribute to the son's wayward-
ness because of his knowledge. To reason otherwise would
be to say that a neglectful father, who takes not the trouble
to study the nature and character of his son, who shuts his
eyes to sinful tendencies, and rests in careless indifference
as to the probable future, will by his very heartlessness be
benefitting his child, because his lack of forethought cannot
operate as a contributory cause to dereliction.

9. Our Heavenly Father has a full knowledge of the
nature and dispositions of each of His children, a knowledge
gained by long observation and experience in the past eternity of our primeval childhood; a knowledge compared with
which that gained by earthly parents through mortal experience with their children is infinitesimally small. By
reason of that surpassing knowledge, God reads the future
of child and children, of men individually and of men collectively as communities and nations; He knows what each
will do under given conditions, and sees the end from the
beginning. His foreknowledge is based on intelligence and
reason; He foresees the future as a state which naturally
and surely will be; not as one which must be because He has
arbitrarily willed that it shall be.

10. But, it may be argued that in the illustrative instance
given above—that of the earthly parent and the wayward

son,—the father had not the power to change the sad course of sin whereby his son is hastening to ignominy and destruction; while the omnipotent Father can save if He will. In reply this is to be said: The Father of souls has endowed His children with the divine birth-right of free agency; He does not and will not control them by arbitrary force; He impels no man toward sin; He compels none to righteousness. Unto man has been given freedom to act for himself; and, associated with this independence, is the fact of strict responsibility and the assurance of individual accountability. In the judgment with which we shall be judged, all the conditions and circumstances of our lives shall be considered. The inborn tendencies due to heredity, the effect of environment whether conducive to good or evil, the wholesome teachings of youth, or the absence of good instruction—these and all other contributory elements must be taken into account in the rendering of a just verdict as to the soul's guilt or innocence. Nevertheless, the divine wisdom makes plain what will be the result with given conditions operating on known natures and dispositions of men; while every individual is free to choose good or evil within the limits of the many conditions existing and operative.[c]

11. Another matter worthy of thought in the present connection is this: Is the fact of the great apostasy,—the virtual overthrow and destruction of the Church established by Jesus Christ,—to be regarded as an instance of failure in the Lord's plans? Is it a case of defeat in which Satan was victor over Christ? Consider the following. What mortal has yet measured the standard by which Omniscience gages success or failure? Who dares affirm that what

---

[c]See Note 2, end of chapter.

man hails as triumph or deplores as defeat will be so accounted when tested by the principles of eternal reckoning?

12.   The history of the world abounds with instances of the temporary triumph of evil, of justice seemingly miscarried, of divine plans for the time being frustrated, of God's purposes opposed and their consummation delayed.

13.   We read of the Lord's covenant with Israel. Unto Abraham, Isaac, and Jacob He declared that their descendants should be a people chosen for His special service among the nations. Through that lineage the Savior of mankind was to be born; in the posterity of Abraham all nations of the earth were to be blessed. Blessings beyond the heart of man to conceive, beyond the mind of man to comprehend, were promised on condition of loyal allegiance to Him who proclaimed Himself their God and their King. Moreover the Lord predicted calamity and suffering, individual affliction and national disgrace, if Israel departed from the service of Jehovah and yielded to the enticements of their heathen neighbors who knew not God. Think you that the Lord was ignorant of the course His people would choose? Did He fail to foresee that Israel would follow the evil way, forfeiting the blessings and reaping the harvest of sorrow? Jehovah's plans failed not, though the realization of the blessings so abundantly promised has been long delayed. Equally forceful with the prediction of calamity in case of sin, was the promise of eventual restoration to favor. The dispersion of Israel already accomplished, was to be followed by the gathering of Israel now in progress.[d]

14.   What would have been the world's verdict as to the success or failure of the mission of the Christ, had a vote

[d]See the author's "Article of Faith," lectures 17 and 18.

been taken at the time of the crucifixion? Seemingly His enemies had triumphed; He who proclaimed Himself the Messiah, the Son of God, the resurrection and the life, over whom death could not prevail, had suffered the fate of malefactors, and His body was in the tomb. But the verdict of the centuries, which is the verdict of the eternities to come, acclaims that "failure" as the greatest triumph of the ages, the victory of victories.

15. Even so with the Church. For a season the powers of evil triumphed, and the spirit of apostasy ruled. But beyond the darkness of the spiritual night the glorious dawn of the restoration was seen in prophetic vision, and both the night with its horrors, and the awakening day with its splendor, were foreseen and foretold.

16. In our study of the predictions of the apostasy as embodied in scripture and of the realization as attested by later history, we shall recognize two distinct phases or stages of the progressive falling away as follows:

(1.) Apostasy *from* the Church; and

(2.) The apostasy *of* the Church.

17. In the first stage we have to deal with the forsaking of the truth and severance from the Church by individuals, at times few, at other times many. Such conditions can scarcely be considered otherwise than as natural and inevitable. History fails to present any example of great undertakings upon which multitudes enter with enthusiasm, and from which many do not desert. Unless such cases of individual abandonment are so numerous as to show the operation of some vital cause of disaffection, we would not need the authority of divine prediction and inspired prophecy to explain the occurrence. We find, however, that apos-

tasy from the Primitive Church was widespread and general, and that the causes leading to such a condition were of vital significance.

18. In the second of the two stages already specified, we are confronted with conditions of far greater import than those attending individual secession from the Church; for here we find the Church sinking to the degraded level of a human institution, with plan of organization and mode of operation foreign to the constitution of the original, without priesthood or authority to officiate in spiritual ordinances, and devoid of the gifts and graces with which the Savior endowed His Church at the time of its establishment. In short, we find the Church itself apostate, boasting of temporal power, making its own laws, teaching its own dogmas, preserving only a form of godliness, while denying the power thereof.[e]

SPECIFIC PREDICTIONS OF THE APOSTASY.

19. The Lord foresaw the great and general departure from the principles of righteousness, and from the beginning knew that men would set up their own forms of worship, wrongfully claiming divine authority for the same. Through the mouths of His chosen prophets He has repeatedly predicted the inevitable event.[f]

20. Among the prophecies antedating the birth of Christ the following may be noted. Isaiah beheld in vision the condition of the earth in the era of spiritual darkness, a period in which all classes would be involved in a general condition of unrighteousness, a time when the world of

[e]See II Tim. 3: 1-6.
[f]See Note 3, end of chapter.

mankind would be in a helpless and practically hopeless condition. He pictures the earth as mourning and languishing in desolation and assigns the reason for the sad condition as follows: "The earth also is defiled under the inhabitants thereof; because they have transgressed the laws, changed the ordinance, broken the everlasting covenant."[g]

21. It may be thought that this prophecy has reference to a violation of the law of Moses under which ancient Israel lived. Let it be remembered, however, that the Mosaic law is nowhere called an everlasting covenant. The covenant between the Lord and Abraham antedated the giving of the law by four hundred and thirty years, and as pointed out by Paul[h] in his epistle to the Galatians, whom he designates as foolish because of their confusing the law of Moses and the gospel of Christ, the law could not nullify the earlier covenant the fulfilment of which could come only through Christ. The "law," by which the inspired apostle plainly means the Mosaic statutes, was but a preparation for the "faith," by which latter expression the gospel as revealed by Christ is clearly intended. "But before faith came," says Paul, "we were kept under the law, shut up unto the faith which should afterwards be revealed. Wherefore the law was our schoolmaster to bring us unto Christ, that we might be justified by faith. But after that faith is come, we are no longer under a schoolmaster. For ye are all the children of God by faith in Jesus Christ. For as many of you as have been baptized into Christ, have put on Christ. There is neither Jew nor Greek, there is neither bond nor free, there is neither male nor female; for ye are

---

[g]Isaiah 24: 5; read verses 1 to 6 inclusive.
[h]Galatians 3: 17; read the entire chapter.

all one in Jesus Christ. And if ye be Christ's then are ye Abraham's seed, and heirs according to the promise."[i]

22.   It is evident from the tenor of the entire chapter, that while the gospel was preached unto Abraham, and covenant made with him relating to the coming of the Messiah through his posterity, the gospel did not abide with Israel, and this because of transgression;[j] but in lieu thereof the Mosaic law was instituted as a disciplinary measure, temporary in character, destined to be superseded by the gospel of Christ, and assuredly not an everlasting covenant. On the other hand, the blood of Christ, through the shedding of which the atoning sacrifice was wrought, is distinctively called "the blood of the everlasting covenant."[k]

23.   It is evident then that Isaiah's fateful prophecy relating to the breaking of the everlasting covenant, could have no reference to a departure from the Mosaic requirements, but must refer to a then future condition of apostasy following the establishment of the everlasting covenant. Moreover, part of the great prediction, referring to the burnings and widespread calamities,[l] yet awaits its complete fulfilment.

24.   Another prediction applicable to the period when there should be no Church of Christ to be found, and when, in consequence there should be lamentation and suffering, is that of Amos: "Behold, the days come, saith the Lord God, that I will send a famine in the land, not a famine of bread, nor a thirst for water, but of hearing the words of the Lord; And they shall wander from sea to sea, and from

---

[i]Verses 23-29.
[j]Verse 19.
[k]Hebrews 13 :20.
[l]See Isaiah 24: 6.

the north even to the east, they shall run to and fro to seek the word of the Lord, and shall not find it."[m]

25. Christ instructed His followers in terms at once direct and conclusive, as to the apostasy then impending. In reply to certain inquiries concerning the signs by which His second advent would be heralded, He said: "Take heed that no man deceive you. For many shall come in my name, saying, I am Christ, and shall deceive many."[n] Then He told of approaching wars and political disturbances, and added "And then shall many be offended and shall betray one another, and shall hate one another. And many false prophets shall rise and shall deceive many. And because iniquity shall abound, the love of many shall wax cold. But he that shall endure unto the end the same shall be saved."[o]

26. Further specifying the conditions incident to the growing apostasy, Christ declared to His disciples: "Then shall they deliver you up to be afflicted, and shall kill you; and ye shall be hated by all nations for my name's sake."[p] And again: "Then if any man shall say unto you, Lo here is Christ, or there, believe it not. For there shall arise false Christs and false prophets, and shall shew great signs and wonders; insomuch that if it were possible they shall deceive the very elect. Behold I have told you before. Wherefore if they shall say unto you, Behold, he is in the desert; go not forth: behold he is in the secret chambers; believe it not."[q]

27. After the departure of Christ from earth His apostles continued to warn the people of the darkness to come.

---

[m] Amos 8: 11, 12.
[n] Matt. 24: 4, 5.
[o] Verses 10-13. See Note 4, end of chapter.
[p] Verse 9.
[q] Verses 23-26.

In that memorable address to the elders at Ephesus, when, as he told them, they were looking upon his face for the last time, Paul reminded his hearers of the instructions he had previously given them, and then charged them with this solemn warning: "For I know this, that after my departing shall grievous wolves enter in among you, not sparing the flock. Also of your own selves shall men arise, speaking perverse things, to draw away disciples after them."[r]

28.   Not only would outsiders ingratiate themselves with the saints for purposes of selfish gain—wolves entering in, and not sparing the flock,—but schisms and divisions were imminent; and these dissensions were to come through some then present—men who would aspire to leadership, and who would set up their own doctrines, thus drawing disciples away from the Church and unto themselves.

29.   The same apostle warns Timothy of the approaching apostasy, and refers to some of the erroneous teachings that would be impressed upon misguided people,— teachings which he calls "doctrines of devils." He admonishes Timothy to put the brethren in remembrance of these things, as is becoming in a good minister of Christ, "nourished up in the words of faith and of good doctrine." Note the inspired prediction: "Now the Spirit speaketh expressly, that in the latter times some shall depart from the faith, giving heed to seducing spirits and doctrines of devils; speaking lies in hypocrisy; having their conscience seared with a hot iron; forbidding to marry, and commanding to abstain from meats, which God hath created to be received with thanksgiving of them which believe and know the truth."[s]

---

[r] Acts 20: 29, 30; read verses 17 to 31 inclusive.
[s] I Tim. 4: 1-3. See Note 5, end of chapter.

30. In a second epistle to his beloved Timothy, while laboring under the premonition that his martyrdom was near at hand, Paul urges zeal and energy in the preaching of the gospel; for the shadows of the apostasy were gathering about the Church. His admonition is pathetic in its earnestness: "I charge thee, before God and the Lord Jesus Christ, who shall judge the quick and the dead at his appearing and his kingdom; Preach the word; be instant in season, out of season; reprove, rebuke, exhort with all longsuffering and doctrine; for the time will come when they will not endure sound doctrine, but after their own lusts shall they heap to themselves teachers having itching ears; and they shall turn away their ears from the truth, and shall be turned unto fables."[t]

31. In addressing the Thessalonian saints, Paul warns them against the error strongly advocated by some that the day of Christ's second advent was then near at hand. It appears that deception was being practiced, and that even forgery was suspected, for the apostle instructs the people that they be not deceived "by word nor by letter as from us." The admonition is forceful: "Now we beseech you, brethren, by the coming of our Lord Jesus Christ, and by our gathering together unto him, That ye be not soon shaken in mind, or be troubled, neither by spirit, nor by word, nor by letter as from us, as that the day of Christ is at hand. Let no man deceive you by any means; for that day shall not come, except there come a falling away first, and that man of sin be revealed, the son of perdition; who opposeth and exalteth himself above all that is called God, or that is worshiped; so that he as God sitteth in the temple of God shewing himself that he is God."[u] We shall see how pain-

'II Tim. 4: 1-4.

fully literal has been the fulfilment of this prophecy in the blasphemous assumptions of the apostate church, centuries later.

32. The Apostle Peter prophesied in language so plain that none may fail to comprehend, concerning the heresies that would be preached as doctrine in the period of the apostasy; and he reminds the people that there were false teachers in olden times, even as there would be in times then future: "But there were false prophets also among the people, even as there shall be false teachers among you, who privily shall bring in damnable heresies, even denying the Lord that bought them, and bring upon themselves swift destruction. And many shall follow their pernicious ways, by reason of whom the way of truth shall be evil spoken of. And through covetousness shall they with feigned words make merchandise of you; whose judgment now of a long time lingereth not, and their damnation slumbereth not."*v*

33. Jude, the brother of James, in his general epistle to the saints, reminds them of earlier warnings: "But beloved, remember ye the words which were spoken before of the apostles of our Lord Jesus Christ. How that they told you there should be mockers in the last time, who should walk after their own ungodly lusts."*w*

34. John, who is called the Revelator, saw in vision the state of the world in the days then future. Describing the spirit of unrighteousness as a hideous beast, and its author, Satan, as the dragon, he says: "And they worshiped the

---

*II Thess. 2: 3, 4.

*II Peter 2: 1-3. Read the entire chapter, noting the description of conditions existing in the world today.

*Jude 17, 18.

dragon which gave power unto the beast: and they worshiped the beast, saying, Who is like unto the beast? who is
able to make war with him? * * * And he opened his
mouth in blasphemy against God, to blaspheme His name,
and His tabernacle, and them that dwell in heaven. And it
was given unto him to make war with the saints, and to
overcome them: and power was given him over all kindreds,
and tongues, and nations. And all that dwell upon the earth
shall worship him, whose names are not written in the book
of life of the Lamb slain from the foundation of the world.
If any man have an ear, let him hear."ᶻ

35.   Note another prophecy based on the vision of John
the Revelator. Again referring to latter-day conditions he
declares: "And I saw another angel fly in the midst of
heaven, having the everlasting gospel to preach unto them
that dwell on the earth, and to every nation, and kindred,
and tongue, and people, Saying with a loud voice, Fear God,
and give glory to him; for the hour of His judgment is
come; and worship Him that made heaven and earth, and
the sea, and the fountains of water."ʸ

36.   While it is true that the scripture last quoted does
not specifically predict the apostasy, the breaking up of the
Church is treated as an event actually accomplished. The
Revelator looked beyond the period of disruption and saw
the brighter day of the restoration of the gospel — a re-
establishment of the Church through the ministry of an
angel. It is illogical to assume that the gospel was to be
brought to earth by a heavenly messenger if that gospel
was still extant upon the earth. Equally unreasonable is it
to say that a restoration or re-establishment of the Church

ᶻRev. 13: 4, 6-9.
ʸRev. 14: 6, 7.

of Christ would be necessary or possible had the Church continued with rightful succession of priesthood and power. If the gospel had to be brought again from the heavens, the gospel must have been taken from the earth. Thus the prophecy of a restoration is proof of an apostasy general and complete.

APOSTASY ON THE WESTERN HEMISPHERE PREDICTED.

37. In the preceding chapter it was shown that the Church of Christ was established by the Risen Lord among the Nephites of the western world. It was foreseen that the powers of evil would be permitted to prevail in the west as in the east. Consider the fateful words of the prophet Alma addressed to his son Helaman: "Behold, I perceive that this very people, the Nephites, according to the spirit of revelation which is in me, in four hundred years from the time that Jesus Christ shall manifest Himself unto them, shall dwindle in unbelief: Yea, and then shall they see wars and pestilences, yea, famines and bloodshed, even until the people of Nephi shall become extinct; Yea, and this because they shall dwindle in unbelief, and fall into the works of darkness, and lasciviousness, and all manner of iniquities; yea, I say unto you that because they shall sin against so great light and knowledge; yea, I say unto you that from that day, even the fourth generation shall not all pass away before this great iniquity shall come."[z]

38. An earlier prophecy relating to the degradation of the surviving remnant of Lehi's descendants, was uttered by Nephi, as a result of a revelation communicated to him through angelic visitation. He thus describes his vision of

---

[z]Alma 45: 10-12.

the future: "I beheld and saw that the seed of my brethren did contend against my seed, according to the word of the angel; and because of the pride of my seed, and the temptations of the devil, I beheld that the seed of my brethren did overpower the people of my seed. And it came to pass that I beheld and saw the people of the seed of my brethren, that they had overcome my seed; and they went forth in multitudes upon the face of the land. And I saw them gathered together in multitudes; and I saw wars and rumors of wars among them; and in wars and rumors of wars I saw many generations pass away. And the angel said unto me: Behold, these shall dwindle in unbelief. And it came to pass that I beheld after they had dwindled in unbelief, they became a dark, and loathsome, and a filthy people, full of idleness and all manner of abominations."* The degraded state of the North American Indians,—descendants of a prophet-father—is a striking realization of this prophetic declaration.

———

39.   The scriptures cited are sufficient to show that widespread apostasy from the Church was foreseen; that the corruption of the Church itself was likewise foreknown; and that on both hemispheres a general apostasy was foretold.

Notes.

1.   THE CHURCH, PRIMITIVE AND RESTORED. The Church of Jesus Christ of Latter-day Saints declares by its name a distinction from the Primitive Church as established by Christ and His early apostles.

———

*I Nephi 12: 19-23. For other Book of Mormon predictions of spiritual decline on the western continent, see II Nephi, 27:1; read also II Nephi 26:19-22, and chapter 29.

The essential designation of the restored Church is the Church of
Jesus Christ; its authorized name is The Church of Jesus Christ of
Latter-day Saints, the final phrase being added to distinguish the
Church as established in the present dispensation from the Church
as organized by the Savior during the period of His earthly ministry.
This distinction is shown in one of our Articles of Faith: "We [the
Church of today] believe in the same organization that existed in the
Primitive Church."

2. MAN'S FREE AGENCY. The teachings of the restored Church
respecting individual freedom of action are thus summarized: "The
Church holds and teaches as a strictly scriptural doctrine, that man
has inherited among the inalienable rights conferred upon him by
his divine Father, absolute freedom to choose the good or the evil
in life as he may elect. This right cannot be guarded with more
jealous care than is bestowed upon it by God Himself: for in all
His dealings with man, He has left the mortal creature free to choose
and to act, with no semblance of compulsion or restraint, beyond the
influences of paternal counsel and loving direction. True, He has
given commandments, and has established statutes, with promises
of blessings for compliance and dire penalties for infraction; but in
the choice of these, God's children are untrammeled. In this respect,
man is no less free than are the angels and the Gods, except as he
has fettered himself with the bonds of sin, and forfeited his power
of will and force of soul. The individual has a full measure of liberty to violate the laws of health, the requirements of nature, and
the commandments of God in matters both temporal and spiritual,
as he has to obey all such; in the one case he brings upon himself
the sure penalties that belong to the broken law; as in the other
he inherits the specific blessings and the added freedom that at-
tend a law-abiding life. Obedience to the law is the habit of the
free man; 'tis the transgressor who fears the law, for he brings upon
himself deprivation and restraint, not because of the law, which
would have protected him in his freedom, but because of his rejection of law. The predominant attribute of justice, recognized as
part of the Divine nature, forbids the thought that man should
receive promises of reward for righteousness, and threats of punish-

ment for evil deeds, if he possessed no power of independent action. It is no more a part of God's plan to compel men to work righteousness, than it is His purpose to permit evil powers to force His children into sin. In the day of Eden, the first man had placed before him commandment and law, with an explanation of the penalty which would follow a violation of that law. No law could have been given him in righteousness, had he not been free to act for himself. 'Nevertheless thou mayest choose for thyself, for it is given unto thee, but remember that I forbid it,' said the Lord God to Adam. Concerning His dealings with the first patriarch of the the race, God has declared in this day, 'Behold I gave unto him that he should be an agent unto himself.'" (The Author, "Articles of Faith," Lecture 3: 1, 2.)

3. THE TESTIMONY OF PROPHECY TO THE APOSTASY. "What is prophecy but history reversed? Nothing. Prophecy is a record of things before they transpire. History is a record of them after they have occurred; and of the two prophecy is more to be trusted for its accuracy than history: for the reason that it has for its source the unerring inspiration of Almighty God; while history—except in the case of inspired historians—is colored by the favor or prejudice of the writer, depends for its exactness upon the point of view from which he looks upon the events; and is likely to be marred in a thousand ways by the influences surrounding him—party considerations, national interest or prejudice; supposed influence upon present conditions and future prospects—all these things may interfere with history; but prophecy is free from such influences. Historians are self-constituted, or appointed by men; but prophets are chosen of God. Selected by divine wisdom, and illuminated by that spirit which shows things that are to come, prophets have revealed to them so much of the future as God would have men to know, and the inspired writers record it for the enlightenment or warning of mankind, without the coloring or distortion so liable to mar the work of the historian. Thus Moses recorded what the history of Israel would be on condition of their obedience to God: and what it would be if they were disobedient. Israel was disobedient, and historians have exhausted their art in attempts to tell of their dis-

obedience and suffering; but neither in vividness nor accuracy do the histories compare with the prophecy. So with the prophecy of Daniel in respect to the rise and succession of the great political powers that should dominate the earth, and the final triumph of the Kingdom of God. So with well-nigh all of the prophecies." (B. H. Roberts, "A New Witness for God," pp. 113, 114.)

4. CHRIST'S PREDICTION OF THE APOSTASY. The forceful prophecy, couched in terms of vivid description, uttered by our Lord in response to inquiries by His disciples, has been the subject of diverse opinion and varied comment, particularly as regards the time to which the prediction refers. As recorded in the twenty-fourth chapter of Matthew, a significant sign of the progress of events to precede the second coming of Christ was stated as follows: "And this gospel of the kingdom shall be preached in all the world for a witness unto all nations; and then shall the end come" (verse 14). It is claimed by many that the "end" referred to in the passage quoted is not necessarily the close of the final dispensation, not what is commonly spoken of as the end of the world, but the closing up of the gospel dispensation then current; and in support of this interpretation it is urged that following the utterance quoted Christ proceeded to predict the calamities then awaiting Jerusalem. That during the period covered by the earthly ministry of the apostles, the gospel was preached in all the civilized nations of the eastern hemisphere, is evident alike from scripture and from the uncanonical writings of repute relating to that period. Paul speaks of the gospel as having been carried in his day to all the world, and as having been preached to every creature under heaven (see Colos. 1: 6, 23; compare Romans 10: 18; see also Note 3, following chapter I of this work, page 15.)

In Joseph Smith's version of the twenty-fourth chapter of Matthew the paragraph relating to the preaching of the gospel in all the world as one of the signs specified by Jesus Christ, is transposed so as to apply more directly to the modern or last dispensation. (See Pearl of Great Price, Writings of Joseph Smith, I.) The scripture under consideration has direct application to the conditions characteristic of present times—the period now current and immediately precedent to the second advent of the Christ. This fact, however, does not necessarily nullify its application to the earlier period as well. History repeats itself in many instances in this, "the dispensation of the fulness of times;" indeed, the very name is expressive of a summarizing or gathering together of things past, and this involves recurrence of earlier conditions and re-enactment of laws. The prediction of world-wide evangelization is not the only instance of a general prophecy having more than a single limited horizon of fulfilment. In the apostolic period the gospel was carried to all nations known to the Lord's ministers; a similar work is in progress today, on a scale greatly exceeding that of the past, for the world, as measured by human occupancy, is vastly greater than of old.

5. SCRIPTURES RELATING TO THE APOSTASY. That the application of the scriptures cited in the text in proof of the predicted apostasy is not peculiar to the Church of Jesus Christ of Latter-day Saints, is shown by the fact that these predictions are similarly interpreted by theologians of other churches. Thus, in his "Bible Commentary," Dr. Adam Clarke annotates Paul's admonition to Timothy as below. First note the passage: "Now the spirit speaketh expressly that in the latter times some shall depart from the faith, giving heed to seducing spirits and doctrines of devils; speaking lies in hypocrisy," etc. Dr. Clarke says:

"*In the latter times*: This does not necessarily imply the last ages of the world; but any times consequent [subsequent] to those in which the church then lived."

"*Depart from the faith*: They will apostatize from the faith, i. e., from Christianity, renouncing the whole system in effect by bringing in doctrines which render its essential truths null and void; or denying and denouncing such doctrines as are essential to Christianity as a system of salvation. A man may hold all the truths of Christianity, and yet render them of none effect, by holding other doctrines, which counteract their influence; or he may apostatize by denying some essential doctrine, though he bring in nothing heterodox."

"*Speaking lies in hypocrisy*: Persons pretending not only to divine inspiration, but also to extraordinary degrees of holiness, self-denial, mortification, etc., in order to credit the lies and false doctrines which they taught. Multitudes of lies were framed concerning miracles wrought by the relics of departed saints as they were termed."

CHAPTER III.

1. As shown in the preceding chapter a general apostasy from the Primitive Church was both foreseen and foretold. Prophets who lived centuries before the time of Christ predicted the great event, as did also the Savior Himself and the apostles who continued the work of the ministry after His resurrection and ascension. We are now to inquire as to the fulfilment of these predictions.

2. Evidence that the apostasy occurred as had been predicted is found in the sacred scriptures and in the records of history other than scriptural. From certain utterances of the early-day apostles it is made plain to us that the great "falling away" had begun even while those apostles were living. The preaching of false doctrines and the rise of unauthorized teachers were referred to as conditions then actually existing in the Church, and not as remote developments of the distant future.[a]

3. Scarcely had the gospel seed been committed to the soil before the enemy came, and by night sowed tares amongst the wheat; and so intimate was the growth of the two that any attempt to forcibly uproot the weeds would have threatened the life of the grain.[b]

4. Paul recognized the fact that the people amongst whom he labored were losing the faith they had professed,

---

[a] See Note 1, end of chapter.
[b] Study the parable of wheat and tares, Matt. 13: 24-30. See Note 2, end of chapter.

and were becoming victims of the deception practiced by
false teachers. In his letter to the churches of Galatia he
wrote: "I marvel that ye are so soon removed from him
that called you into the grace of Christ unto another gospel:
Which is not another; but there be some that trouble you,
and would pervert the gospel of Christ." And then, to emphasize the sin of those who thus sought to "pervert the
gospel of Christ," he continued: "But though we, or an
angel from heaven, preach any other gospel unto you than
that which we have preached unto you, let him be accursed.
As we said before, so say I now again, If any man preach
any other gospel unto you than that ye have received, let
him be accursed."[c]

5.   The context of the passages just quoted shows the
nature of the error into which "the churches of Galatia"
were in danger of falling. They were embroiled in a discussion as to whether they were bound by certain requirements of the law of Moses, notably that respecting circumcision. The apostle instructs them to the effect that the
gospel of Christ was superior to the law; and that moreover, they were inconsistent in contending for one item of
the law and neglecting the rest. We have here indication
of the effort so persisted in even by those who had joined
the Church, to modify and change the simple requirements
of the gospel by introducing the elements of Judaism. It
must be remembered that even among the apostles some
difference of opinion had existed as to the necessity of circumcision; but this had been settled by their prayerful effort to learn the Lord's will in the matter; and those who
sought to foment dissension on this or any other matter

---

[c]Galatians 1: 6-9; read the entire chapter. See Note 3, end of
chapter.

of authoritative doctrine were declared to be enemies to the Church, seeking to "pervert the gospel of Christ."

6.   In his second epistle to the "church of the Thessalonians" Paul declares that the spirit of iniquity was then already operative. After predicting the rise of the apostate church, with its blasphemous assumptions of power, as a condition antecedent to the second coming of Christ, the apostle continued as follows: "For the mystery of iniquity doth already work: only he who now letteth will let, until he be taken out of the way. And then shall that Wicked be revealed, whom the Lord shall consume with the spirit of His mouth, and shall destroy with the brightness of His coming."[d]

7.   The seemingly obscure expression, "he who now letteth will let," may be more readily understood by remembering that in the older style of English "let" had the meaning of "restrain" or "hinder."[e] The passage therefore may be understood as a declaration that the spirit of iniquity was already active though restrained or hindered for a time; and that later even this restraint would be removed and the evil one would be in power. In the Revised Version of the New Testament this passage is rendered thus: "—lawlessness doth already work: only there is one that restraineth now, until he be taken out of the way."

8.   Just who or what is referred to as exercising a restraint on the powers of iniquity at that time has given rise to discussion. Some writers hold that the presence of the apostles operated in this way, while others believe that the

---

[d] II Thess. 2: 7, 8.

[e] An example of this old-time use of the verb "let" is found in Shakespeare. Hamlet is made to say, "Unhand me, gentlemen. By heaven I'll make a ghost of him who lets me," i. e., of him who restrains or hinders me.

restraining power of the Roman government is referred to. It is known that the Roman policy was to discountenance religious contention, and to allow a large measure of liberty in forms of worship as long as the gods of Rome were not maligned nor their shrines dishonored. As Roman supremacy declined "the mystery of iniquity" embodied in the apostate church operated practically without restraint.

9.   The expression "mystery of iniquity" as used by Paul is significant.[f] Prominent among the early perverters of the Christian faith were those who assailed its simplicity and lack of exclusiveness. This simplicity was so different from the mysteries of Judaism and the mysterious rites of heathen idolatry as to be disappointing to many; and the earliest changes in the Christian form of worship were marked by the introduction of mystic ceremonies.

10.   Paul's zeal as a missionary and a proselyter is abundantly shown in scripture; he was equally zealous in seeking to maintain the faith of those who had accepted the truth. The Pauline epistles abound in admonitions and pleadings against the increasing influence of false doctrines, and in expressions of sorrow over the growth of apostasy in the Church. His words addressed to Timothy are both emphatic and pathetic: "Hold fast the form of sound words, which thou hast heard of me, in faith and love which is in Christ Jesus. That good thing which was committed unto thee keep by the Holy Ghost, which dwelleth in us. This thou knowest, *that all they which are in Asia be turned away from me.*"[g]

11.   An excellent summary of important utterances by the Apostle Paul relating to the beginning of the apostasy

---

[f]See Note 1, end of chapter.
[g]II Timothy 1: 13-15; Italics introduced; compare 4: 10, 16.

as a fact in the early apostolic age, has been made by one of the latter-day apostles, Orson Pratt. He writes as follows: "The great apostasy of the Christian Church commenced in the first century; while there were yet inspired apostles and prophets in their midst; hence Paul, just previous to his martyrdom, enumerates a great number who had 'made shipwreck of their faith,' and 'turned aside unto vain jangling;' teaching 'that the resurrection was already past,' giving 'heed to fables and endless genealogies,' 'doubting about questions and strifes of words whereof came envyings, railings, evil surmisings, perverse disputings of men of corrupt minds and destitute of the truth, supposing that gain is godliness.' This apostasy had become so general that Paul declares to Timothy, 'that all they which are in Asia be turned away from me;' and again he says, 'at my first answer no man stood with me, but all men forsook me;' he further says that 'there are many unruly, and vain talkers, deceivers, teaching things which they ought not, for filthy lucre's sake.' These apostates, no doubt, pretended to be very righteous; for, says the apostle, 'they profess that they know God: but in words they deny Him, being abominable and disobedient and unto every good work reprobate.' "

12. Jude admonished the saints to be on their guard against men who were in the service of Satan seeking to corrupt the Church. Addressing himself "to them that are sanctified by God the Father and preserved in Jesus Christ," he said: "It was needful for me to write unto you, and exhort you that ye should earnestly contend for the faith which was once delivered unto the saints. For there are certain men crept in unawares, who were before of old ordained to this condemnation, ungodly men, turning the grace of our God into lasciviousness, and denying the only

Lord God, and our Lord Jesus Christ."[h] It is plain that Jude
considered "the faith which was once delivered unto the
saints" as in danger; and he urges the faithful to contend for
it and openly defend it. He reminds the saints that they had
been told "there should be mockers in the last time, who
should walk after their own ungodly lusts;" and adds
"These be they who separate themselves, sensual, having
not the Spirit."[i] Clearly he is referring to the apostates of
the time, who, because of sensual appetites and lustful de-
sires, had separated themselves from the Church.

13.   During the banishment of John the Revelator on the
isle of Patmos, when nearly all the apostles had been taken
from the earth, many of them having suffered martyrdom,
the apostasy was so wide-spread that only seven "churches,"
i. e. branches of the Church, remained in such condition as
to be considered deserving of the special communication
John was instructed to give. In a marvelous vision he beheld the seven churches typified by seven golden candle-
sticks, with seven stars representing the presiding officers of
the several churches; and in the midst of the golden candle-
sticks, with the stars in his hand, stood "one like unto the
Son of Man."

14.   The church at Ephesus was approved for its good
works, specifically for its rejection of the Nicolaitan heresies; nevertheless reproof was administered for disaffection
and neglect, thus:—"thou hast left thy first love. Remember therefore from whence thou art fallen, and repent
and do the first works; or else I will come unto thee quickly,
and will remove thy candlestick out of his place, except thou
repent."[j]

---

[h]Jude 3, 4. See Note 5, end of chapter.
[i]Verses 18, 19.
[j]Revelation 2: 4, 5.

15. To the church at Pergamos John was commanded to write, denouncing the false doctrines of certain sects and teachers, "which thing I hate" said the Lord.[k] The church of the Laodiceans was denounced as "lukewarm," neither hot nor cold," and as priding itself as rich and not in need, whereas it was in reality "wretched, and miserable, and poor, and blind, and naked."[l]

16. The foregoing scriptures are ample as proof that even before the ancient apostles had finished their earthly ministry, apostasy was growing apace. The testimony of the early "Christian fathers" who wrote in the period immediately following the passing of the apostles, is to the same effect. According to the generally accepted chronology, the prophetic message of John the Revelator to the churches of Asia was given in the last years of the first century.[m]

17. Among the historians of that period whose writings are not regarded as canonical or scriptural, but which are nevertheless accepted as genuine and reliable, was Hegesippus, who, "flourished nearest the days of the apostles." Writing of the conditions marking the close of the first century and the beginning of the second, Eusebius cites the testimony of the earlier writer as follows: — "The same author, [Hegesippus] relating the events of the times, also says, that the Church continued until then as a pure and uncorrupt virgin; whilst if there were any at all that attempted to pervert the sound doctrine of the saving gospel, they were yet skulking in dark retreats; but when the sacred choir of apostles became extinct, and the generation of those that had been privileged to hear their inspired wisdom had

[k]See verses 12-16.
[l]Rev. 3; see verses 14-21.
[m]Probably about A. D. 96; see Oxford Bible, margin.

passed away, then also the combinations of impious error
arose by the fraud and delusions of false teachers. These
also, as there were none of the apostles left, henceforth attempted, without shame to preach their false doctrine
against the gospel of truth. Such is the statement of Hegesippus."ⁿ

18.   There can be little doubt that the false teachers referred to in the testimony last cited, were professed adherents of the Church, and not outside opponents, inasmuch as
they were restrained by the influence and authority of the
apostles, and waited the passing of the authorized leaders
as an opportunity to corrupt the Church by evil teachings.

19.   A later writer commenting on the schisms and dissensions by which the Church was rent in the latter part of
the first century—the period immediately following that of
the apostolic ministry, says: "It will easily be imagined that
unity and peace could not reign long in the Church, since
it was composed of Jews and Gentiles, who regarded each
other with the bitterest aversion. Besides, as the converts
to Christianity could not extirpate radically the prejudices
which had been formed in their minds by education, and
confirmed by time, they brought with them into the bosom
of the church more or less of the errors of their former religions. Thus the seeds of discord and controversy were easily sown, and could not fail to spring up soon into animos-
ities and dissensions, which accordingly broke out and
divided the Church."º

20.   Another recognized authority on ecclesiastical history, and one whose avowed purpose was to present the

---

*Eusebius, "Ecclesiastical History," Book III, chapter 32.
°Mosheim, "Eccl. History," Cent. I, Part II; chapter 3: 11. See
Note 4, end of chapter.

truth respecting the Church in its most favorable light, is Joseph Milner, author of a comprehensive "History of the Church of Christ." He comments on the state of the Church at the close of the first century in this wise: "Let us keep in view what that [the spirit of the gospel] really is. The simple faith of Christ as the only Savior of lost sinners, and the effectual influences of the Holy Ghost in recovering souls altogether depraved by sin—these are the leading ideas. When the effusion of the Holy Ghost first took place, these things were taught with power; and no sentiments which militated against them could be supported for a moment. As, through the prevalence of human corruption and the crafts of Satan, the love of truth was lessened, heresies and various abuses of the gospel appeared; and in estimating them we may form some idea of the declension of true religion toward the end of the [first] century." The same writer continues: "Yet a gloomy cloud hung over the conclusion of the first century. The first impressions made by the effusion of the Spirit are generally the strongest and the most decisively distinct from the spirit of the world. But human depravity, over-born for a time, arises afresh, particularly in the next generation. Hence the disorders of schism and heresy. Their tendency is to destroy the pure work of God."[p]

———

21. The purpose of this chapter has been that of demonstrating the early beginning of the apostasy, so soon to become general, and later, universal. The specific causes directly contributing to the degradation of the Church are reserved for future consideration.

———

[p]Milner, "Church History," Cent. I, ch. 15.

22.   Now let us see what was the condition of the Church established by the Resurrected Lord among the descendants of Lehi on the American continent. In this undertaking we shall not restrict ourselves to the beginning of the disruption alone.   Inasmuch as the course of apostasy among the Nephites was so rapid, and the period intervening between the establishment of the Church and the destruction of the nation was so brief, we shall consider the history of the Church to its close, and thus obviate the necessity of recurring to the subject in later chapters.   We read that the Church had prospered until about 200 A. D.   Then apostasy became general, as evidence of which note the following:

23.   "And now in this two hundred and first year, there began to be among them those who were lifted up in pride * * * And they began to be divided into classes, and they began to build up churches unto themselves, to get gain, and began to deny the true Church of Christ.   And it came to pass that when two hundred and ten years had passed away there were many churches in the land: yea, there were many churches which professed to know the Christ, and yet they did deny the more parts of his gospel, insomuch that they did receive all manner of wickedness, and did administer that which was sacred unto him to whom it had been forbidden because of unworthiness.   And this church did multiply exceedingly, because of iniquity, and because of the power of Satan who did get hold upon their hearts.   And again, there was another church which denied the Christ, and they did persecute the true Church of Christ because of their humility and their belief in Christ; and they

did despise them because of the many miracles which were wrought among them."[q]

24. The Book of Mormon record is definite in its specifications of the immediate reasons for, or causes of the great apostasy on the western hemisphere. While the members of the Church remained faithful to their covenants and obligations, they as individuals and the Church as an organization prospered; and their enemies were unable to prevail against them. With prosperity, however, came pride and class distinctions, the rich dominated the poor, and earthly gain became the object of life.[r] Secret organizations of evil purpose flourished;[s] the people were divided into two opposing factions, those who still professed a belief in Christ being known as Nephites and their enemies as Lamanites, without regard to actual descent or family relationship. With the growth of pride and its attendant sins, the Nephites became as wicked as the non-professing Lamanites;[t] and in their wickedness these people sought each other's destruction. Consider the pathos and dire tragedy expressed in the words of Moroni, the solitary survivor of a once blessed and mighty nation:

25. "Behold, four hundred years have passed away since the coming of our Lord and Savior. And behold, the Lamanites have hunted my people, the Nephites, down from city to city, and from place to place, even until they are no more, and great has been their fall: yea, great and marvelous is the destruction of my people, the Nephites. And behold, it is the hand of the Lord which hath done it. And

---

[q]IV Nephi 24-29; read the entire chapter.

[r]See IV. Nephi 2-7 and compare with verses 25, 26.

[s]Verse 42.

[t]Verse 45.

behold also, the Lamanites are at war one with another; and
the whole face of this land is one continual round of murder
and bloodshed; and no one knoweth the end of the war. And
now behold, I say no more concerning them, for there are
none save it be the Lamanites and robbers that do exist
upon the face of the land; and there are none that do know
the true God save it be the disciples of Jesus,[u] who did tarry
in the land until the wickedness of the people was so great
that the Lord would not suffer them to remain with the people; and whether they be upon the face of the land no man
knoweth."[v]

Notes.

1. THE EARLY APOSTASY RECOGNIZED. That fact of the early beginning of the apostasy is generally recognized by theologians and
authorities on biblical interpretation. Clarke's commentary on the
declaration of Paul as to the "mystery of iniquity" then at work
(See I Thess. 2: 7) is as follows:

"For the mystery of iniquity doth already work: There is a system
of corrupt doctrine which will lead to the *general apostasy, already
in existence; but it is a mystery;* it is as yet hidden; it dare not show
itself because of that which hindereth or withholdeth. But when
that which now restraineth is taken out of the way, then shall that
wicked one be revealed; it will then be manifest 'who he is and
what he is."

2. EARLY DISSENSIONS IN THE CHURCH. As instances of the dis-
agreements and differences that troubled and disturbed the Church
even in apostolic days Mosheim says: "The first of these controversies, which was set on foot in the church of Antioch, regarded
the necessity of observing the law of Moses, and its issue is mentioned by St. Luke in the Acts of the Apostles (chap. 15). This
controversy was followed by many others, either with the Jews who
were violently attached to the worship of their ancestors, or with

---

"See III Nephi 28: 1-7.
"Mormon 8: 6-10.

the votaries of a wild and fanatical sort of philosophy, or with such as, mistaking the true genius of the Christian religion, abused it monstrously to the encouragement of their vices, and their indulgence of the appetites and passions. St. Paul and the other apostles have, in several places of their writings, mentioned these controversies, but with such brevity that it is difficult at this distance of time to come at the true state of the question in these various disputes. The most weighty and important of all these controversies was that which certain Jewish doctors raised at Rome, and in other Christian churches concerning the means of justification and acceptance with God, and the method of salvation pointed out in the word of God. The apostles, wherever they exercised their ministry, had constantly declared all hopes of acceptance and salvation delusive, except such as were founded on Jesus the Redeemer, and his all-sufficient merits; while the Jewish doctors maintained the works of the law to be the true efficient cause of the soul's eternal salvation and felicity. This latter sentiment not only led to many other errors extremely prejudicial to Christianity, but was also injurious to the glory of the divine Savior." (Mosheim, "Ecclesiastical History," Cent. I, Part II, 11: 12.)

3. UNAUTHORIZED WRITINGS IN THE APOSTOLIC AGE. Paul's reference to "another gospel" in his epistle to the Galatians (1:6) suggested to Dr. Adam Clarke the following commentary on the passage:

"*Another gospel*: It is certain that in the very earliest ages of the Christian Church, there were several spurious gospels in circulation; and it was the multitude of these false or inaccurate relations that induced St. Luke to write his own (see Luke 1: 1). We have the names of more than seventy of these spurious narratives still on record, and in ancient writers many fragments of them remain; these have been collected and published by Fabricius in his account of the apocryphal books of the New Testament (3 vols, 8 vo.) In some of these gospels the necessity of circumcision and subjection to the Mosaic law, in unity with the gospel, were strongly inculcated." (Clarke, "Bible Commentary.")

4. SOME AUTHORITIES ON ECCLESIASTICAL HISTORY. Among the authorities cited in the text are those named below. A brief note as to each may be of interest.

Eusebius: Eusebius Pamphilus, bishop of Caesarea in Palestine. He lived from about 260 to about 339 A. D., though there is some uncertainty as to the exact time of his death. He was an eyewitness of and a participant in some of the sufferings incident to heathen persecution of the Christians, and has been called the "Father of Church History." He was the author of several works, among them one of the earliest on "Ecclesiastical History." The quotations from this work by Eusebius, as given in the text, are from the version translated from the Greek by C. F. Cruse.

Mosheim: Dr. J. L. von Mosheim, chancellor of the University of Göttingen; a German writer, noted for his contributions to church history. He is the author of an exhaustive work on "Ecclesiastical History" (6 vols.), dated 1755. The excerpts from Mosheim's "Ecclesiastical History" given in the text are taken from the version translated into English by Dr. Archibald Maclaine, dated 1764.

Milner: Rev. Joseph Milner. An English authority on church history, and author of a comprehensive "History of the Church of Christ" (5 vols.), from which the excerpts in the text are taken.

5. COMMENTARY ON THE PASSAGE FROM JUDE: — The passage quoted in the text—"For there are certain men crept in unawares, *who were before of old ordained to this condemnation,* ungodly men," etc. (Jude: 4), has given rise to discussion, the question at issue being as to whether the principle of pre-appointment or foreordination is here involved. A hasty and casual reading of the passage may suggest the inference that the "ungodly men" referred to had been appointed or "ordained" in the providence of God to sow the seeds of discord and dissension in the Church. A careful study of this scripture shows that no such inference is warranted. The "ungodly men" "who were before of old ordained to this condemnation" were men who had already, i. e., previously, been denounced, proscribed and condemned for the very heresies which now they were endeavoring to perpetuate in the Church, they having crept in unawares, or in other words, they having become members by false pretenses and profession, and being able because of their membership, to spread their false teachings more effectively. Dr. Adam Clarke, in his Bible Commentary, thus treats the passage under consideration:

"For there are certain men crept in unawares." They have got into the church under specious pretenses, and when in, began to sow their bad seed.

"Before of old ordained: Such as were long ago proscribed and condemned in the most public manner; this is the import of the [original] word in this place, and there are many examples of this use of it in the Greek writers."

"To this condemnation: To a similar punishment to that about to be mentioned.

"In the sacred writings all such persons, false doctrines and impure practices have been most openly proscribed and condemned, and the apostle immediately produces several examples, viz., the disobedient Israelites, the unfaithful angels, and the impure inhabitants of Sodom and Gomorrah. This is most obviously the apostle's meaning, and it is ridiculous as it is absurd, to look into such words for a decree of reprobation, etc., such a doctrine being as far from the apostle's mind as from that of Him in whose name he wrote." (Clarke, "Bible Commentary," Jude 4.)

In the Revised Version of the New Testament the passage is rendered thus: "I was constrained to write unto you, exhorting you to contend earnestly for the faith which was once for all delivered unto the saints. For there are certain men crept in privily, even they who were of old set forth unto this condemnation, ungodly men, turning the grace of our God into lasciviousness, and denying our only Master and Lord, Jesus Christ.

CHAPTER IV.

1.   We are now to consider some of the principal causes contributing to apostasy from the Primitive Church and leading later to the apostasy of the Church as an earthly institution; and we are to study the manner in which those causes have operated.

2.   In the scriptures before cited as proof of the early beginning of the apostasy, many of the contributing causes are indicated, such as the rise of false teachers, the spread of heretical doctrines, and the growth of the power of Satan in general. These may be classed as internal causes, originating within the Church itself. In contrast with these there were other conditions operating upon the Church from without; and such may be classed as external causes. For convenience in study we shall consider the subject in the following order of treatment: (1) External causes; (2) Internal causes.

EXTERNAL CAUSES OF THE GREAT APOSTASY.

3.   External conditions operating against the Church, tending to restrict its development and contributing to its decline may be designated by the general term, *persecution*. It is a matter of history, undisputed and indisputable, that from the time of its inception to that of its actual cessation, the Church established by Jesus Christ was the object of bitter persecution, and the victim of violence. The question as to whether persecution is to be regarded as an ele-

ment tending to produce apostasy is worthy of present consideration. Opposition is not always destructive; on the
contrary it may contribute to growth. Persecution may im-
pel to greater zeal, and thus prove itself a potent factor of
advancement. A proverb still in favor declares that "the
blood of the martyrs is the seed of the Church." But prov-
erbs and adages, aphorisms and parables, while true as gen-
eralities, are not always applicable to special conditions.

4. Undoubtedly the persistent persecution to which the
early Church was subjected caused many of its adherents
to renounce the faith they had professed and to return to
their former allegiances, whether Judaistic or pagan. Church
membership was thus diminished; but such instances of
apostasy from the Church may be regarded as individual
desertions and of comparatively little importance in its
effect upon the Church as a body. The dangers that affrighted some would arouse the determination of others;
the ranks deserted by disaffected weaklings would be replenished by zealous converts. Let it be repeated that apostasy from the Church is insignificant as compared with the
apostasy of the Church as an institution. Persecution as
a cause of apostasy has operated indirectly but none the less
effectively upon the Church of Christ.[a]

5. We have considered briefly the testimony of early
church historians showing that schism, contention, and perversion of doctrine invaded the Church immediately after
the passing of the apostles; we have seen how wolves had
awaited the departure of the shepherds that they might the
more effectively worry the flock. It cannot be denied that
the early persecutions were directed most particularly
against the leaders of the people; the sharpest shafts were

---

[a]See Notes 1 and 2, end of chapter.

aimed against the officers of the Church. In the fierce battle
between Christianity and its allied foes—Judaism and heath-
endom—the strong men who stood for Christ were the first
to fall. And with their fall, the traitors within the Church,
the ungodly and the rebellious, those who had crept in unawares, and whose sinister purpose it was to pervert the
gospel of Christ, were relieved of restraint, and found themselves free to propagate their heresies and to undermine the
foundations of the Church. Persecution, operating from
without, and therefore essentially an external cause, served
to set in motion the enginery of disruption within the
Church, and therefore must be treated as an effective element contributing to the great apostasy.

6. A further purpose in introducing here a brief summary of the persecutions of which the early Church was the
victim, is that of affording a basis of ready comparison between such and the persecutions waged by the apostate
church itself in later centuries. We shall find that the sufferings of the Church in the days of its integrity, are sur-
passed by the cruel inflictions perpetrated in the name of
Christ. Moreover, a study of the early persecutions will
enable us to contrast the conditions of opposition and pov-
erty with those of ease and affluence as affecting the integrity of the Church and the devotion of its adherents.

7. The persecution to which the Primitive Church was
subjected was two-fold; viz. Judaistic and pagan. It must
be remembered that the Jews were distinguished from all
other nations of antiquity by their belief in the existence
of a living God. The rest of the world before and at the
time of Christ was idolatrous and pagan, professedly believing in a host of deities, yet with no recognition of a Supreme Being as a living personage. The Jews were bitter

in their opposition to Christianity, which they regarded as
a rival religion to their own; and moreover, they recognized
the fact that if Christianity ever came to be generally accepted as the truth, their nation would stand convicted of
having put to death the Messiah.

JUDAISTIC PERSECUTION.[b]

8. Opposition to Christianity on the part of those who
belonged to the House of Israel was rather Judaistic than
Jewish. The conflict was between systems, not between
peoples or nations. Christ was a Jew: His apostles were
Jews, and the disciples who constituted the body of the
Church at its establishment and throughout the early years
of its existence were largely Jews. Our Lord's instructions
to the chosen twelve on their first missionary tour restricted
their ministry to the House of Israel;[c] and when the time
was propitious for extending the privileges of the gospel to
the Gentiles, a miraculous manifestation was necessary to
convince the apostles that such extension was proper.[d] The
Church was at first exclusively and for a long time pre-
eminently Jewish in membership. Judaism, the religious
system founded on the law of Moses, was the great enemy
of Christianity. When therefore we read of the Jews opposing the Church, we understand that Judaistic Jews are
meant—defenders of Judaism as a system, upholders of the
law and enemies of the gospel. With this explanation of
the distinction between the Jews as a people and Judaism
as a system, we may employ the terms "Jews" and "Jewish"

---

[b]See Note 3, end of chapter.
[c]See Matt. 10: 5, 6.
[d]See Acts chapters 10 and 11.

according to common usage, keeping in mind, however, the true signification of the terms.

9. Judaistic opposition to the Church was predicted. While Jesus ministered in the flesh He specifically and repeatedly warned the apostles of the persecution they would have to meet. In answering certain inquiries Christ said to Peter and others: "But take heed to yourselves: for they shall deliver you up to councils; and in the synagogues ye shall be beaten; and ye shall be brought before rulers and kings for my sake for a testimony against them."*e*

10. Shortly before His betrayal the Lord repeated the warning with solemn impressiveness, citing the persecutions to which He had been subject, and declaring that His disciples could not escape: "If the world hate you, ye know that it hated me before it hated you. If ye were of the world the world would love his own; but because ye are not of the world, but I have chosen you out of the world, therefore the world hateth you. Remember the word that I said unto you, The servant is not greater than his lord. If they have persecuted me they will also persecute you."*f*

11. The extreme of depravity to which the bigoted persecutors would sink is set forth in these further words of the Savior: "They shall put you out of the synagogues: yea, the time cometh, that whosoever killeth you will think that he doeth God service. And these things will they do unto you because they have not known the Father, nor me."*g*

12. These predictions had speedy and literal fulfilment. From the time of the crucifixion, Jewish malignity and

---

*e*Mark 13: 9; compare Matt. 10: 16-18; 24: 9-13; Luke 21: 12.

*f*John 15: 18-20.

*g*John 16: 2, 3; compare 9: 22, and 12: 42.

hatred were directed against all who professed a belief in
the divinity of Jesus Christ. In the early stages of their
ministry several of the apostles were imprisoned[h] and the
priestly leaders sought to take their lives.[i] Stephen was
stoned to death because of his testimony;[j] and the persecution against the Church became general.[k] James, the son
of Zebedee, was slain by order of Herod,[l] and Peter was
saved from a similar fate only by a miraculous intervention.[m]
The scriptural record informs us as to the ultimate fate of
but few of the apostles; and secular history is likewise in-
complete. That Peter would be numbered with the martyrs
was made known by the resurrected Lord.[n] Paul sets forth
the fact that the apostles lived in the very shadow of death[o]
and that persecution was their heritage.[p]

13. Not only did the Jews wage relentless persecution
against those of their number who professed Christ, but
they sought to stir up opposition on the part of the Romans,
and to accomplish this end charged that the Christians were
plotting treason against the Roman government. Even during the personal ministry of the early apostles, persecution
of the saints had spread from Jerusalem, throughout Palestine and into the adjacent provinces. In this evil work the
Jews sought to incite their own people living in the outlying
parts, and also to arouse the opposition of the officers and
rulers of the Roman dominions. As evidence of this phase
of the persecution, partly Jewish and partly pagan, insti-

[h]Acts 5: 18; compare 4: 3.
[i]Acts 5: 33.
[j]See Acts 6: 8-15; 7: 54-60.
[k]See Acts 8: 1.
[l]Acts 12: 1, 2.
[m]Verses 3-10.
[n]See John 21: 18, 19.
[o]I Cor. 4: 9.
[p]Verses 11-13; see also II Cor. 4: 8, 9; 6: 4, 5.

gated by Jews and participated in by others, the following
quotation from Mosheim may suffice:

14. "The Jews who lived out of Palestine, in the Roman
provinces, did not yield to those of Jerusalem in point of
cruelty to the innocent disciples of Christ. We learn from
the history of the Acts of the Apostles, and other records
of unquestionable authority, that they spared no labor, but
zealously seized every occasion of animating the magistrates against the Christians, and setting on the multitude
to demand their destruction. The high priest of the nation
and the Jews who dwelt in Palestine were instrumental in
inciting the rage of these foreign Jews against the infant
Church, by sending messengers to exhort them, not only to
avoid all intercourse with the Christians, but also to persecute them in the most vehement manner. For this inhuman
order they endeavored to find out the most plausible pre-
texts; and therefore, they gave out, that the Christians were
enemies to the Roman emperor, since they acknowledged
the authority of a certain person whose name was Jesus,
whom Pilate had punished capitally as a malefactor by a
most righteous sentence, and on whom, nevertheless, they
conferred the royal dignity."[q]

15. In the latter half of the first century, the scene of
Judaistic persecution of the Church had shifted from Jerusalem to the outlying provinces; and the cause of this was
the general exodus of Christians from the city whose destruction had been decreed.[r] Our Lord's predictions as to
the fate of Jerusalem and His warnings to the people[s] had

---

[q]Mosheim, "Ecclesiastical History," Cent. I, Part I, 5: 2.
[r]See Note 4, end of chapter.
[s]See Luke 21: 5-9, 20-24.

been very generally heeded. Eusebius[1] informs us that the body of the Church had moved from Jerusalem into the provinces beyond the Jordan, and thus largely escaped the calamities of the Jews who remained.

Notes.

1. PERSECUTION IN DIFFERENT DISPENSATIONS. It may be argued that, judging from the history of the re-established Church in the present dispensation, persecution may tend to strengthen rather than to weaken the Church, and that therefore violent opposition in earlier times cannot be considered a true cause leading to final disruption. In reply it may be said that the present is the dispensation of the fulness of times,—a period in which the Church shall triumph, and during which the powers of evil are limited and restrained in their opposition; whereas the period of the apostasy was one of temporary victory for Satan. Our belief in the eventual triumph of good over evil must not blind us to the fact that evil is frequently allowed a short-lived success, and a seeming victory. The permanency of the Latter-day Church has been not less surely predicted than was the temporary duration of the Primitive Church. Satan was given power to overcome the saints in former days, and the persecutions he waged against them and the officers of the Church contributed to his passing success. It has been decreed that he shall not have power to destroy the Church in the last dispensation, and his persecution of the saints today will be futile as a means of bringing about a general apostasy in these latter times.

2. PERSECUTION AS A POSSIBLE CAUSE OF APOSTASY. "Let it not be a matter of surprise that I class those persecutions as among the means through which the church was destroyed. The force of heathen rage was aimed at the leaders and strong men of the body religious; and being long-continued and relentlessly cruel, those most steadfast in their adherence to the Church invariably became its victims. These being stricken down, it left none but weaklings to contend for the faith, and made possible those subsequent innovations in the religion of Jesus which a pagan public sentiment demanded, and which so completely changed both the spirit and form of the Christian religion as to subvert it utterly. Let me further ask that no

[1]Eusebius, "Ecclesiastical History," Book III, ch. 5.

one be surprised that violence is permitted to operate in such a case. The idea that the right is always victorious in this world, that truth is always triumphant and innocence always divinely protected, are old, fond fables with which well-meaning men have amused credulous multitudes; but the stern facts of history and actual experience in life correct the pleasing delusion. Do not misunderstand me. I believe in the ultimate victory of the right, the ultimate triumph of truth, the final immunity of innocence from violence. These—innocence, truth and the right—will be at the last more than conquerors; they will be successful in the war, but that does not prevent them from losing some battles. It should be remembered always that God has given to man his agency; and that fact implies that one man is as free to act wickedly as another is to do righteousness. Cain was as free to murder his brother as that brother was to worship God; and so the pagans and Jews were as free to persecute and murder the Christians as the Christians were to live virtuously and worship Christ as God. The agency of man would not be worth the name if it did not grant liberty to the wicked to fill the cup of their iniquity, as well as liberty to the virtuous to round out the measure of their righteousness. Such perfect liberty or agency God has given man; and it is only so variously modified as not to thwart his general purposes." (B. H. Roberts, "A New Witness for God," pp. 47, 48.)

3. EARLY PERSECUTIONS BY THE JEWS. "The innocence and virtue that distinguished so eminently the lives of Christ's servants, and the apostles' purity of the doctrine they taught, were not sufficient to defend them against the virulence and malignity of the Jews. The priests and rulers of that abandoned people not only loaded with injuries and reproach the apostles of Jesus and their disciples, but condemned as many of them as they could to death, and executed in the most irregular and barbarous manner their decrees. The murder of Stephen, of James, the son of Zebedee, and of James surnamed the Just, bishop of Jerusalem, furnished dreadful examples of the truth of what we here advance. This odious malignity of the Jewish doctors against the heralds of the gospel, was undoubtedly owing to a secret apprehension that the progress of Christianity would destroy the credit of Judaism, and bring on the ruin of their pompous ceremonies." In a footnote to the foregoing, references appear as follows: "The martyrdom of Stephen is re-

corded in the Acts of the Apostles 7: 55; and that of James, the son of Zebedee, Acts 12: 1, 2, and that of James the Just, bishop of Jerusalem, is mentioned by Josephus in his Jewish Antiquities, book XX, chap. 8; and by Eusebius in his Ecclesiastical History, book II, chap. 23." (Mosheim, "Ecclesiastical History," Cent. I, Part I, 5: 1.)

4. DESTRUCTION OF JERUSALEM BY THE ROMANS. "A rebellious disturbance among the Jews gave a semblance of excuse for a terrible chastisement to be visited upon them by their Roman masters, which culminated in the destruction of Jerusalem (A. D. 71.) The city fell after a six months' siege before the Roman arms led by Titus, son of the Emperor Vespasian. Josephus, the famous historian, to whom we owe most of our knowledge as to the details of the struggle, was himself a resident of Galilee and was carried to Rome among the captives. From his record we learn that nearly a million Jews lost their lives through the famine incident to the siege; many more were sold into slavery, and uncounted numbers were forced into exile. The city was utterly destroyed, and the site upon which the temple had stood was plowed up by the Romans in their search for treasure. Thus literally were the words of Christ fulfilled, 'There shall not be left here one stone upon another that shall not be thrown down.' (Matt. 24; 1, 2; see also Luke 19: 44.)" (The Author, "The Articles of Faith," Lecture 17: 18.)

CHAPTER V

1. As already pointed out, it is convenient to study the causes leading to the great apostasy as belonging to two classes, external and internal, or (1) causes due to conditions operating against the Church from without; and (2) causes arising from dissension and heresy within the Church itself. We have summarized external causes under the general term persecution; and we have drawn a distinction between Judaistic and pagan persecution waged against the Church. Having dealt with the opposition suffered by the early Christians at the hands of the Jews or through Jewish instigation, we have now to consider the persecution brought upon the believers in Christ by pagan nations.

PAGAN PERSECUTION.

2. The term "pagan" as here used may be taken as a synonym of "heathen," and is to be understood as referring to persons or peoples who did not believe in the existence of the living God, and whose worship was essentially idolatrous. The motives impelling non-believing Jews to oppose the establishment and spread of Christianity may readily be understood, in view of the fact that the religion taught by Christ appeared as a rival to Judaism, and that the growth and spread of the one meant the decline if not the extinction of the other. The immediate motive leading to bitter and widespread persecution of the Christians by heathen peoples is not so easy to perceive, since there was no uniform system of idolatrous worship in any single nation, but a vast di-

versity of deities and cults of idolatry, to no one of which was Christianity opposed more than to all. Yet we find the worshipers of idols forgetting their own differences and uniting in opposition to the gospel of peace,—in persecution waged with incredible ferocity and indescribable cruelty.[a]

3.   Unfortunately, historians differ widely in their records of persecution of Christians, according to the point of view from which each writer wrote. Thus, in a general way, Christian authors have given extreme accounts of the sufferings to which the Church and its adherents individually were subjected; while non-Christian historians have sought to lessen and minimize the extent and severity of the cruelties practiced against the Christians. There are facts, however, which neither party denies, and to which both give place in their separate records. To make a fair interpretation of these facts, drawing just and true inferences therefrom, should be our purpose.

4.   Among pagan persecutors of the Church, the Roman empire is the principal aggressor. This may appear strange in view of the general tolerance exercised by Rome toward her tributary peoples; indeed, the real cause of Roman opposition to Christianity has given rise to many conjectures. It is probable that intolerant zeal on the part of the Christians themselves had much to do with their unpopularity among heathen nations. This subject is conservatively summed up by Mosheim as follows:

5.   "A very natural curiosity calls us to inquire, how it happened that the Romans, who were troublesome to no nation on account of their religion, and who suffered even the

---

[a]See Note 1, end of chapter.

Jews to live under their own laws, and follow their own methods of worship, treated the Christians alone with such severity. This important question seems still more difficult to be solved, when we consider, that the excellent nature of the Christian religion, and its admirable tendency to promote both the public welfare of the state, and the private felicity of the individual, entitled it, in a singular manner, to the favor and protection of the reigning powers. One of the principal reasons of the severity with which the Romans persecuted the Christians, notwithstanding these considerations, seems to have been the abhorrence and contempt with which the latter regarded the religion of the empire, which was so intimately connected with the form, and indeed, with the very essence of its political constitution. For, though the Romans gave an unlimited toleration to all religions which had nothing in their tenets dangerous to the commonwealth, yet they would not permit that of their ancestors, which was established by the laws of the state, to be turned into derision, nor the people to be drawn away from their attachment to it. These, however, were the two things which the Christians were charged with, and that justly, though to their honor. They dared to ridicule the absurdities of the pagan superstition, and they were ardent and assiduous in gaining proselytes to the truth. Nor did they only attack the religion of Rome, but also all the different shapes and forms under which superstition appeared in the various countries where they exercised their ministry. From this the Romans concluded, that the Christian sect was not only insupportably daring and arrogant, but, moreover, an enemy to the public tranquility, and every way proper to excite civil wars and commotions in the empire. It is, probably on this account that Tacitus reproaches them with the odious character of haters of mankind, and styles the religion of Jesus as destructive superstition; and that Suetonius speaks of the Christians and their doctrine in terms of the same kind.

6. "Another circumstance that irritated the Romans against the Christians, was the simplicity of their worship, which resembled in nothing the sacred rites of any other people. The Christians had neither sacrifices, nor temples, nor images, nor oracles, nor sacerdotal orders; and this was sufficient to bring upon them the reproaches of an ignorant multitude, who imagined that there could be no religion without these."[b]

7. Persecution of the Church by Roman authority may be said to have begun in the reign of Nero (A. D. 64) and to have continued to the close of Diocletian's reign (A. D. 305). Within this range of time there were many periods of diminished severity, if not of comparative tranquility; nevertheless, the Church was the object of heathen oppression for about two and a half centuries. Attempts have been made by Christian writers to segregate the persecutions into ten distinct and separate onslaughts; and some profess to find a mystic relation between the ten persecutions thus classified, and the ten plagues of Egypt, as also an analogy with the ten horns mentioned by John the Revelator.[c] As a matter of fact attested by history, the number of persecutions of unusual severity was less than ten; while the total of all, including local and restricted assaults, would be much greater.[d]

---

[b]Mosheim, "Eccl. Hist." Cent. I, Part I, ch. 5: 6, 7.
[c]See Rev. 17: 14.
[d]See Note 2, end of chapter.

8. *Persecution under Nero.* The first extended and notable persecution of Christians under the official edict of a Roman emperor was that instigated by Nero, A. D. 64. As students of history know, this monarch is remembered mostly for his crimes. During the latter part of his infamous reign, a large section of the city of Rome was destroyed by fire. He was suspected by some of being responsible for the disaster; and, fearing the resentment of the infuriated people, he sought to implicate the unpopular and much-maligned Christians as the incendiaries, and by torture tried to force a confession from them. As to what followed the foul accusation, let us consider the words of a non-Christian writer, Tacitus, whose integrity as a historian is held in esteem.

9. "With this view, he [Nero] inflicted the most exquisite tortures on those men who, under the vulgar appellation of Christians, were already branded with deserved infamy. They derived their name and origin from Christ, who, in the reign of Tiberius had suffered death by the sentence of the procurator Pontius Pilate. For a while this dire superstition was checked; but it again burst forth; and not only spread itself over Judea, the first seat of this mischievous sect, but was even introduced into Rome, the common asylum which receives and protects whatever is impure, whatever is atrocious. The confessions of those that were seized discovered a great multitude of their accomplices, and they were all convicted, not so much for the crime of setting fire to the city, as for their hatred of human kind. They died in torments, and their torments were embittered by insults and derision. Some were nailed on crosses; other sewn up in the skins of wild beasts and exposed to the fury of dogs; others, again, smeared over with

combustible materials, were used as torches to illuminate
the darkness of the night. The gardens of Nero were destined for the melancholy spectacle, which was accompanied
with a horse-race, and honored with the presence of the
emperor, who mingled with the populace in the dress and
attitude of a charioteer. The guilt of the Christians deserved indeed the most exemplary punishments, but the
public abhorrence was changed into commiseration, from
the opinion that those unhappy wretches were sacrificed,
not so much to the public welfare as to the cruelty of a
jealous tyrant."[e]

10.   There is some disagreement among historians as
to whether the Neronian persecution is to be regarded as
a local infliction, practically confined to the city of Rome,
or as general throughout the provinces.[f] The consensus of
opinion favors the belief that the provinces followed the example of the metropolis, and that the persecution was common throughout the Church.

11.   This, the first persecution by Roman edict, practically
ended with the death of the tyrant Nero A. D. 68. According to tradition handed down from the early Christian writers, the Apostles Paul and Peter suffered martyrdom at
Rome, the former by beheading, the latter by crucifixion,
during this persecution, and is further stated that Peter's
wife was put to death shortly before her husband; but the
tradition is neither confirmed nor disproved by authentic
record.

12.   *Persecution under Domitian.* The second officially
appointed persecution under Roman authority began 93
or 94 A. D. in the reign of Domitian. Both Christians and

---

[e]Tacitus, Annals, Book 15, ch. 44.
[f]See Note 3, end of chapter.

Jews came under this prince's displeasure, because they refused to reverence the statues he had erected as objects of adoration. A further cause for his special animosity against the Christians, as affirmed by early writers, is as follows. The emperor was persuaded that he was in danger of losing his throne, in view of a reputed prediction that from the family to which Jesus belonged there would arise one who would weaken if not overthrow the power of Rome. With this as his ostensible excuse, this wicked ruler waged terrible destruction on an innocent people. Happily, the persecution thus started was of but few years duration. Mosheim and others aver that the end of the persecution was caused by the emperor's untimely death; though Eusebius, who wrote in the fourth century, quotes an earlier writer as declaring that Domitian had the living descendants of the Savior's family brought before him, and that after questioning them he became convinced that he was in no danger from them; and thereupon dismissed them with contempt and ordered the persecution to cease. It is believed that while the edict of Domitian was in force the Apostle John suffered banishment to the isle of Patmos.

13. *Persecution under Trajan.* What is known in ecclesiastical history as the third persecution of the Christian Church took place in the reign of Trajan, who occupied the imperial throne from 98 to 117 A. D. He was and is regarded as one of the best of the Roman emperors, yet he sanctioned violent persecution of the Christians owing to their "inflexible obstinacy" in refusing to sacrifice to Roman gods. History has preserved to us a very important letter asking instructions from the emperor, by the younger Pliny, who was governor of Pontus, and the emperor's reply thereto. This correspondence is instructive as showing the

extent to which Christianity had spread at that time, and the way in which believers were treated by the officers of the state.

14.   Pliny inquired of the emperor as to the policy to be pursued in dealing with the Christians within his jurisdiction. Were young and old, tender and robust, to be treated alike, or should punishment be graded? Should opportunity be given the accused to recant, or was the fact that they had once professed Christianity to be considered an unpardonable offense? Were those convicted as Christians to be punished for their religion alone, or only for specific offenses resulting from their membership in the Christian Church? After propounding such queries the governor proceeded to report to the emperor what he had done in the absence of definite instructions. In reply the emperor directed that the Christians were not to be hunted nor sought after vindictively, but if accused and brought before the judgment seat, and if then they refused to renounce their faith, they were to be put to death.[g]

15.   *Persecution under Marcus Aurelius.* Marcus Aurelius reigned from 161 to 180 A. D. He was noted as one who sought the greatest good of his people; yet under his government the Christians suffered added cruelties. Persecution was most severe in Gaul (now France.) Among those who met the martyr's fate at that time, were Polycarp, bishop of Smyrna, and Justin Martyr, known in history as the philosopher. With reference to the seeming anomaly that even the best rulers permitted and even prosecuted vigorous opposition to Christian devotees, as exemplified by the acts of this emperor, a modern writer has said: "It should be noted that the persecution of the Christians under

[g]See Note 4, end of chapter.

the pagan emperors sprung from political rather than religious motives, and that is why we find the names of the best emperors, as well as those of the worst, in the list of persecutors. It was believed that the welfare of the state was bound up with the careful performance of the rites of the national worship; and hence, while the Roman rulers were usually very tolerant, allowing all forms of worship among their subjects, still they required that men of every faith should at least recognize the Roman gods, and burn incense before their statues. This the Christians steadily refused to do. Their neglect of the service of the temple, it was believed, angered the gods, and endangered the safety of the state, bringing upon it drought, pestilence, and every disaster. This was the main reason of their persecution by the pagan emperors."[h]

16. *Later persecutions.* With occasional periods of partial cessation, the Christian believers continued to suffer at the hands of heathen opponents throughout the second and third centuries. A violent persecution marked the reign of Severus (193-211 A. D.) in the first decade of the third century; another characterized the reign of Maximin (235-238 A. D.) A period of unusual severity in persecution and suffering befell the Christians during the short reign of Decius known also as Decius Trajan (249-251 A. D.) The persecution under Decius is designated in ecclesiastical history as the seventh persecution of the Christian Church. Others followed in rapid succession. Some of these periods of specific oppression we pass over and come to the consideration of the

17. *Diocletian persecution,* which is spoken of as the tenth, and happily the last. Diocletian reigned from 284 to

[h]General History by P. V. N. Myers, edition of 1889, p. 322.

305 A. D. At first he was very tolerant toward Christian belief and practice; indeed it is of record that his wife and daughter were Christians, though "in some sense, secretly." Later, however, he turned against the Church and undertook to bring about a total suppression of the Christian religion. To this end he ordered a general destruction of Christian books, and decreed the penalty of death against all who kept such works in their possession.

18. Fire broke out twice in the royal palace at Nicomedia, and on each occasion the incendiary act was charged against the Christians with terrible results. Four separate edicts, each surpassing in vehemence the earlier decrees, were issued against the believers; and for a period of ten years they were the victims of unrestrained rapine, spoliation, and torture. At the end of the decade of terror the Church was in a scattered and seemingly in a hopeless condition. Sacred records had been burnt; places of worship had been razed to the ground; thousands of Christians had been put to death; and every possible effort had been made to destroy the Church and abolish Christianity from the earth. Descriptions of the horrible extremes to which brutality was carried are sickening to the soul. A single example must suffice. Eusebius, referring to the persecutions in Egypt, says: "And such too was the severity of the struggle which was endured by the Egyptians, who wrestled gloriously for the faith at Tyre. Thousands, both men, and women and children, despising the present life for the sake of our Savior's doctrine, submitted to death in various shapes. Some, after being tortured with scrappings and the rack, and the most dreadful scourgings, and other innumerable agonies which one might shudder to hear, were finally committed to the flames; and some plunged and

drowned in the sea, others voluntarily offering their own heads to their executioners, others dying in the midst of their torments, some wasted away by famine, and others again fixed to the cross. Some, indeed, were executed as malefactors usually were; others, more cruelly, were nailed with the head downwards, and kept alive until they were destroyed by starving on the cross itself."[i]

19. A modern writer, whose tendency ever was to minimize the extent of Christian persecution, is Edward Gibbon. His account of the conditions prevailing during this period of Diocletian outrage is as follows: "The magistrates were commanded to employ every method of severity which might reclaim them from their odious superstition, and oblige them to return to the established worship of the gods. This rigorous order was extended, by a subsequent edict, to the whole body of Christians, who were exposed to a violent and general persecution. Instead of those salutary restraints which had required the direct and solemn testimony of an accuser, it became the duty as well as the interest of the imperial officers to discover, to pursue, and to torment the most obnoxious among the faithful. Heavy penalties were denounced against all who should presume to save a proscribed sectary from the just indignation of the gods and of the emperors."[j]

20. So general was the Diocletian persecution, and so destructive its effect, that at its cessation the Christian Church was thought to be forever extinct. Monuments were raised to commemorate the emperor's zeal as a persecutor, notably two pillars erected in Spain. On one of them is an

[i]Eusebius, "Eccl. Hist.," Book 8, ch. 8.
[j]Gibbon, "Decline and Fall of the Roman Empire," ch. XVI.

inscription extolling the mighty Diocletian *"For having extinguished the name of Christians who brought the Republic to ruin."* A second pillar commemorates the reign of Diocletian, and honors the imperator *"for having everywhere abolished the superstition of Christ; for having extended the worship of the gods."* A medal struck in honor of Diocletian bears the inscription *"The name of Christian being extinguished."*[k] To the fallacy of these assumptions subsequent events testify.

21.   The Diocletian oppression was the last of the great persecutions brought by pagan Rome against Christianity as a whole. A stupendous change, amounting to a revolution, now appears in the affairs of the Church. Constantine, known in history as Constantine the Great, became emperor of Rome A. D. 306, and reigned 31 years. Early in his reign he espoused the hitherto unpopular cause of the Christians, and took the Church under official protection. A legend gained currency that the emperor's conversion was due to a supernatural manifestation, whereby he saw a luminous cross appear in the heavens with the inscription, "By this sign, conquer." The genuineness of this alleged manifestation is doubtful, and the evidence of history is against it. The incident is here mentioned to show the means devised to make Christianity popular at the time.

22.   It is held by many judicious historians that Constantine's so-called conversion was rather a matter of policy than a sincere acceptance of the truth of Christianity. The emperor himself remained a *catechumen,* that is, an unbaptized believer, until shortly before his death, when he became a member by baptism. But, whatever his motives may

---

[k]Milner, "Church History," Cent. IV., ch. 1: 38.

have been, he made Christianity the religion of state, issuing an official decree to this effect in 313. " He made the cross the royal standard; and the Roman legions now for the first time marched beneath the emblem of Christianity" (Myers).

23.   Immediately following the change there was great competition for church preferment. The office of a bishop came to be more highly esteemed than the rank of a general. The emperor himself was the real head of the Church. It became unpopular and decidedly disadvantageous in a material sense to be known as a non-Christian. Pagan temples were transformed into churches, and heathen idols were demolished. We read that twelve thousand men and a proportionate number of women and children were baptized into the Church at Rome alone within a single year. Constantine removed the capital of the empire from Rome to Byzantium, which city he re-named after himself, Constantinople. This, the present capital of Turkey, became headquarters of the state Church.

24.   How empty and vain appears the Diocletian boast that Christianity was forever extinguished! Yet how different was the Church under the patronage of Constantine from the Church as established by Christ and as built up by His apostles! The Church had already become apostate as judged by the standard of its original constitution.

Notes.

1.   CAUSE OF PAGAN OPPOSITION TO CHRISTIANITY. "The whole body of Christians unanimously refused to hold any communion with the gods of Rome, of the empire, and of mankind. It was in vain that the oppressed believer asserted the inalienable rights of conscience and private judgment. Though his situation might excite

the pity, his arguments could never reach the understanding, either of the philosophic or of the believing part of the pagan world. To their apprehensions, it was no less a matter of surprise that any individuals should entertain scruples against complying with the established mode of worship, than if they had conceived a sudden abhorrence to the manners, the dress, or the language of their native country. The surprise of the pagans was soon succeeded by resentment; and the most pious of men were exposed to the unjust but dangerous imputation of impiety. Malice and prejudice concurred in representing the Christians as a society of atheists, who, by the most daring attack on the religious constitution of the empire, had merited the severest animadversion of the civil magistrate. They had separated themselves (they gloried in the confession) from every mode of superstition which was received in any part of the globe by the various temper of polytheism; but it was not altogether so evident what deity or what form of worship they had substituted to the gods and temples of antiquity. The pure and sublime idea which they entertained of the Supreme Being escaped the gross conception of the pagan multitude, who were at a loss to discover a spiritual and solitary God, that was neither represented under any corporeal figure or visible symbol, nor was adored with the accustomed pomp of libations and festivals, of altars and sacrifices." (Gibbon, "Decline and Fall of the Roman Empire," chap. XVI.)

2. AS TO THE NUMBER OF PERSECUTIONS BY THE ROMANS. "The Romans are said to have pursued the Christians with the utmost violence in ten persecutions, but this number is not verified by the ancient history of the church. For if, by these persecutions, such only are meant as were singularly severe and universal throughout the empire, then it is certain that these amount not to the number above mentioned. And, if we take the provincial and less remarkable persecutions into the account, they far exceed it. In the fifth century, certain Christians [were] led by some passages of the holy scriptures and by one especially in the Revelations (Rev. 17: 14), to imagine that the church was to suffer ten calamities of a most grievous nature. To this notion, therefore, they endeavored, though not all in the same way, to accommodate the language, even against the testimony of those ancient records, from whence alone history can speak with authority." (Mosheim, "Ecclesiastical History," Cent. I, Part I: ch. 5: 4.)

Speaking on the same subject, Gibbon says: "As often as any occasional severities were exercised in the different parts of the empire, the primitive Christians lamented and perhaps magnified their own sufferings; but the celebrated number of ten persecutions has been determined by the ecclesiastical writers of the fifth century, who possessed a more distinct view of the prosperous or adverse fortunes of the church from the age of Nero to that of Diocletian. The ingenious parallels of the ten plagues of Egypt and of the ten horns of the Apocalypse first suggested this calculation to their minds; and in their application of the faith of prophecy to the truth of history they were careful to select those reigns which were indeed the most hostile to the Christian cause." (Gibbon, "Decline and Fall of the Roman Empire," ch. XVI.)

3. EXTENT OF THE NERONIAN PERSECUTION. "Learned men are not entirely agreed concerning the extent of this persecution under Nero. Some confine it to the city of Rome, while others represent it as having raged throughout the whole empire. The latter opinion, which is also the most ancient, is undoubtedly to be preferred; as it is certain that the laws enacted against the Christians were enacted against the whole body, and not against particular churches, and were consequently in force in the remotest provinces." (Mosheim, "Ecclesiastical History," Cent. I, Part I, 5: 14.)

4. CORRESPONDENCE BETWEEN PLINY AND TRAJAN. The inquiry of the younger Pliny, governor of Pontus, addressed to Trajan, emperor of Rome, and the imperial reply thereto, are of such interest as to be worthy of reproduction in full. The version here given is that of Milner as appears in his "History of the Church of Christ," edition of 1810, Cent. II, ch. 1.

"Pliny to Trajan, Emperor:

"Health.—It is my usual custom, Sir, to refer all things, of which I harbor any doubts, to you. For who can better direct my judgment in its hesitation, or instruct my understanding in its ignorance? I never had the fortune to be present at any examination of Chris-

tians, before I came into this province. I am therefore at a loss to
determine what is the usual object either of inquiry or of punishment, and to what length either of them is to be carried. It has
also been with me a question very problematical,—whether any distinction should be made between young and the old, the tender
and the robust;—whether any room should be given for repentance,
or the guilt of Christianity once incurred is not to be expiated by
the most unequivocal retraction; — whether the name itself, ab-
stracted from any flagitiousness of conduct, or the crimes connected
with the name, be the object of punishment. In the meantime,
this has been my method, with respect to those who were brought
before me as Christians. I asked them whether they were Christians:
if they pleaded guilty, I interrogated them twice afresh with a men-
ace of capital punishment. In case of obstinate perseverence I
ordered them to be executed. For of this I had no doubt, whatever
was the nature of their religion, that a sudden and obstinate inflexi-
bility called for the vengeance of the magistrate. Some were infected
with the same madness, whom, on account of their privilege of
citizenship, I reserved to be sent to Rome, to be referred to your
tribunal. In the course of this business, informations pouring in, as
is usual when they are encouraged, more cases occurred. An anonymous libel was exhibited, with a catalogue of names of persons,
who yet declared that they were not Christians then, nor ever had
been; and they repeated after me an invocation of the gods and
of your image, which, for this purpose, I had ordered to be brought
with the images of the deities. They performed sacred rites with
wine and frankincense, and execrated Christ,—none of which things
I am told a real Christian can ever be compelled to do. On this
account I dismissed them. Others named by an informer, first affirmed, and then denied the charge of Christianity; declaring that
they had been Christians, but had ceased to be so some three years
ago, others even longer, some even twenty years ago. All of them
worshiped your image, and the statues of the gods, and also exe-

crated Christ. And this was the account which they gave of the nature of the religion they had once professed, whether it deserves the name of crime or error,—namely—that they were accustomed on a stated day to meet before daylight, and to repeat among themselves a hymn to Christ as to a god, and to bind themselves by an oath, with an obligation of not committing any wickedness;—but on the contrary, of abstaining from thefts, robberies, and adulteries; —also of not violating their promise or denying a pledge;—after which it was their custom to separate, and to meet again at a promiscuous harmless meal, from which last practice they however desisted, after the publication of my edict, in which, agreeably to your orders, I forbade any societies of that sort. On which account I judged it the more necessary to inquire, by torture, from two females, who were said to be deaconesses, what is the real truth. But nothing could I collect except a depraved and excessive superstition. Deferring, therefore, any farther investigation, I determined to consult you. For the number of culprits is so great as to call for serious consultation. Many persons are informed against of every age and of both sexes; and more still will be in the same situation. The contagion of the superstition hath spread not only through cities, but even villages and the country. Not that I think it impossible to check and correct it. The success of my endeavors hitherto forbids such desponding thoughts; for the temples, once almost desolate, began to be frequented, and the sacred solemnities, which had long been intermitted, are now attended afresh; and the sacrificial victims are now sold everywhere, which once could scarcely find a purchaser. Whence I conclude that many might be reclaimed were the hope of impunity, on repentance, absolutely confirmed."

The emperor's reply follows:

"Trajan to Pliny:

"You have done perfectly right, my dear Pliny, in the inquiry which you have made concerning Christians. For truly no one general rule can be laid down, which will apply to all cases. These people must not be sought after. If they are brought before you and convicted, let them be capitally punished, yet with this restriction, that if any one renounce Christianity, and evidence his sincerity by supplicating our gods, however suspected he may be for the past, he shall obtain pardon for the future, on his repentance. But anonymous libels in no case ought to be attended to; for the precedent would be of the worst sort, and perfectly incongruous to the maxims of my government."

CHAPTER VI.

1. The cruel persecution to which the adherents of Christianity and the Church as an organized body were subjected during the first three centuries of our era have been treated as external causes, contributing at least indirectly to the general apostasy. Details of Judaistic and heathen opposition have been given with sufficient fulness to show that the unpopular Church had a troubled existence, and that such of its members as remained faithful to the tenets and principles of the gospel were martyrs in spirit if not in fact.

2. As would naturally be expected, the immediate effect of persistent persecution on those who professed a belief in the divinity of the Lord Jesus was diverse and varied; indeed it ranged from unrestrained enthusiasm expressed in frenzied clamoring for martyrdom, to ready and abject apostasy with ostentatious display of devotion in idolatrous service.

3. Many of the Christian devotees developed a zeal amounting to mania, and, disregarding all prudence and discretion, gloried in the prospect of winning the martyr's crown. Some who had been left unassailed felt themselves aggrieved, and became their own accusers; while others openly committed acts of aggression with intent to bring resentment upon themselves.[a] These extravagances were doubtless encouraged by the excessive veneration accorded the memories and the bodily remains of those who had

---

[a] See Note 1, end of chapter.

fallen as victims in the cause. The reverential respect so rendered developed later into the impious practice of martyr worship.

4. Commenting on the imprudent enthusiasm of the early Christians, Gibbon says: "The Christians sometimes supplied by their voluntary declaration the want of an accuser, rudely disturbed the public service of paganism, and, rushing in crowds round the tribunal of the magistrates, called upon them to pronounce and to inflict the sentence of the law. The behavior of the Christians was too remarkable to escape the notice of the ancient philosophers; but they seem to have received it with much less admiration than astonishment. Incapable of conceiving the motives which sometimes transported the fortitude of believers beyond the bounds of prudence and reason, they treated such an eagerness to die as the strange result of obstinate despair, of stupid insensibility or of superstitious frenzy."[b]

5. But there is another side to the picture. While imprudent zealots invited dangers from which they might have remained exempt, others, affrighted at the possibility of being included among the victims, voluntarily deserted the Church and returned to heathen allegiances. Milner, speaking of conditions existing in the third century, and incorporating the words of Cyprian, bishop of Carthage, who lived at the time of the incident described, says: "Vast numbers lapsed into idolatry immediately. Even before men were accused as Christians, many ran to the forum and sacrificed to the gods as they were ordered; and the crowds of apostates were so great, that the magistrates wished to delay numbers of them till the next day, but they were impor-

---

[b]Gibbon, "Decline and Fall of the Roman Empire," ch. XVI.

tuned by the wretched suppliants to be allowed to prove themselves heathens that very night."[c]

6. In connection with this individual apostasy of Church members under the pressure of persecution, there arose among the provincial governors a practice of selling certificates or "libels" as these documents were called, which "attested that the persons therein mentioned had complied with the laws and sacrificed to the Roman deities. By producing these false declarations, the opulent and timid Christians were enabled to silence the malice of an informer, and to reconcile, in some measure, their safety with their religion."[d] A modification of this practice of quasi-apostasy consisted in procuring testimonials from persons of standing certifying that the holders had abjured the gospel; these documents were presented to the heathen magistrates, and they, on receipt of a specified fee, granted exemption from the requirement of sacrificing to the pagan gods.[e] As a result of these practices, whereby under favorable circumstances the wealthy could purchase immunity from persecution, and at the same time maintain a semblance of standing in the Church, much dissension arose, the question being as to whether those who had thus shown their weakness could ever be received again into communion with the Church.

7. Persecution at most was but an indirect cause of the decline of Christianity and the perversion of the saving principles of the gospel of Christ. The greater and more immediate dangers threatening the Church must be sought within the body itself. Indeed, the pressure of opposition

---

[c]Milner, "Church History," Cent. III, ch. 8.
[d]Gibbon, "Decline and Fall of the Roman Empire," ch. XVI.
[e]See Milner, "Church History," Cent. III. ch. 9.

from without served to restrain the bubbling springs of internal dissension, and actually delayed the more destructive eruptions of schism and heresy.[f] A general review of the history of the Church down to the end of the third century shows that the periods of comparative peace were periods of weakness and decline in spiritual earnestness, and that with the return of persecution came an awakening and a renewal in Christian devotion. Devout leaders of the people were not backward in declaring that each recurring period of persecution was a time of natural and necessary chastisement for the sin and corruption that had gained headway within the Church.[g]

8. As to the condition of the Church in the middle of the third century, Cyprian, the bishop of Carthage, thus speaks: "If the cause of our miseries be investigated, the cure of the wound may be found. The Lord would have his family to be tried. And because long peace had corrupted the discipline divinely revealed to us, the heavenly chastisement hath raised up our faith, which had lain almost dormant: and when, by our sins, we had deserved to suffer still more, the merciful Lord so moderated all things, that the whole scene rather deserves the name of a trial than a persecution. Each had been bent on improving his patrimony; and had forgotten what believers had done under the apostles, and what they ought always to do:—they were brooding over the arts of amassing wealth:—the pastors and the deacons each forgot their duty: Works of mercy were neglected, and discipline was at the lowest ebb. —Luxury and effeminacy prevailed: Meretricious arts in dress were cultivated: Frauds and deceit were practiced among brethren.—Christians could unite themselves in

[f]See Note 2, end of chapter.
[g]See Note 3, end of chapter.

matrimony with unbelievers; could swear not only without reverence, but even without veracity. With haughty asperity they despised their ecclesiastical superiors: They railed against one another with outrageous acrimony, and conducted quarrels with determined malice:—Even many bishops, who ought to be guides and patterns to the rest, neglecting the peculiar duties of their stations, gave themselves up to secular pursuits:—They deserted their places of residence and their flocks: They traveled through distant provinces in quest of pleasure and gain; gave no assistance to the needy brethren; but were insatiable in their thirst of money:—They possessed estates by fraud and multiplied usury. What have we not deserved to suffer for such a conduct? Even the divine word hath foretold us what we might expect.— 'if his children forsake my law, and walk not in my judgments, I will visit their offenses with the rod, and their sin with scourges.' These things had been denounced and foretold, but in vain. Our sins had brought our affairs to that pass, that because we had despised the Lord's directions, we were obliged to undergo a correction of our multiplied evils and a trial of our faith by severe remedies."[h]

9. Milner, who quotes approvingly the severe arraignment of the Church in the third century as given above, cannot be charged with bias against Christian institutions, inasmuch as his declared purpose in presenting to the world an additional "History of the Church of Christ" was to give due attention to certain phases of the subject slighted or neglected by earlier authors, and notably to emphasize the piety, not the wickedness, of the professed followers of Christ. This author, avowedly friendly to the Church and her votaries, admits the growing depravity of the Christian

---

[h]As quoted by Milner, "Church History," Cent. III, ch. 8.

sect, and declares that toward the end of the third century
the effect of the Pentecostal outpouring of the Holy Spirit
had become exhausted, and that there remained little proof
of any close relationship between Christ and the Church.

10.   Note his summary of conditions: "The era of its actual declension must be dated in the pacific part of Diocletian's reign. During this whole century the work of God,
in purity and power, had been tending to decay. The connection with philosophers was one of the principal causes.
Outward peace and secular advantages completed the corruption. Ecclesiastical discipline, which had been too strict,
was now relaxed exceedingly; bishops and people were in
a state of malice. Endless quarrels were fomented among
contending parties, and ambition and covetousness had in
general gained the ascendency in the Christian Church.
* * * The faith of Christ itself appeared now an ordinary
business; and here *terminated*, or nearly so, as far as appears, that first great effusion of the Spirit of God, which
began at the day of Pentecost. Human depravity effected
throughout a general decay of godlines; and one generation
of men elapsed with very slender proofs of the spiritual
presence of Christ with His Church."[i]

11.   If further evidence be wanted as to the fires of disaffection smoldering within the Church, and so easily
fanned into destructive flame, let the testimony of Eusebius
be considered with respect to conditions characterizing the
second half of the third century. And, in weighing his
words, let it be remembered that he had expressly recorded
his purpose of writing in defense of the Church, and in
support of her institutions. He bewails the tranquility preceding the Diocletian outbreak, because of its injurious

---

'Milner, "Church History," Cent. III, ch. 17.

effect upon both officers and members of the Church. These are his words: "But when by excessive liberty we sunk into indolence and sloth, one envying and reviling another in different ways, and we were almost, as it were, on the point of taking up arms against each other, and were assailing each other with words, as with darts and spears, prelates inveighing against prelates, and people rising up against people, and hypocrisy and dissimulation had arisen to the greater heights of malignity, then the divine judgment, which usually proceeds with a lenient hand, whilst the multitudes were yet crowding into the Church, with gentle and mild visitations began to afflict its episcopacy; the persecution having begun with those brethren that were in the army. * * * But some that appeared to be our pastors, deserting the law of piety, were inflamed against each other with mutual strifes, only accumulating quarrels and threats, rivalry, hostility, and hatred to each other, only anxious to assert the government as a kind of sovereignty for themselves."[j]

12. As further illustrative of the decline of the Christian spirit toward the end of the third century, Milner quotes the following observation of Eusebius, an eye-witness of the conditions described: "The heavy hand of God's judgments began softly, by little and little, to visit us after his wonted manner; * * * but we were not at all moved with his hand, nor took any pains to return to God. We heaped sin upon sin, judging like careless Epicureans, that God cared not for our sins, nor would ever visit us on account of them. And our pretended shepherds, laying aside the rule of godliness, practiced among themselves contention and division." He adds that the "dreadful persecution

---

[j]Eusebius, "Ecclesiastical History, Book VIII, ch. 1. See Note 4, end of chapter.

of Diocletian was then inflicted on the Church as a just punishment, and as the most proper chastisement for their iniquities."[k]

13. It will be remembered that the great change whereby the Church was raised to a place of honor in the state, occurred in the early part of the fourth century. It is a popular error to assume that the decay of the Church as a spiritual institution dates from that time. The picture of the Church declining as to spiritual power in exact proportion to her increase of temporal influence and wealth has appealed to rhetoricians and writers of sensational literature; but such a picture does not present the truth. The Church was saturated with the spirit of apostasy long before Constantine took it under his powerful protection by according it official standing in the state. In support of this statement, I quote again from Milner, the avowed friend of the Church: "I know it is common for authors to represent the great declension of Christianity to have taken place only after its external establishment under Constantine. But the evidence of history has compelled me to dissent from this view of things. In fact we have seen that for a whole generation previous to the [Diocletian] persecution, few marks of superior piety appeared. Scarcely a luminary of godliness existed; and it is not common in any age for a great work of the Spirit of God to be exhibited but under the conduct of some remarkable saints, pastors, and reformers. This whole period as well as the whole scene of the persecution is very barren in such characters. * * * Moral and philosophical and monastical instructions will not effect for men what is to be expected from evangelical doctrine. And if the faith of Christ was so much declined (and its decayed

---

[k]Milner, "Church History," Cent. III, ch. 17.

state ought to be dated from about the year 270), we need not wonder that such scenes as Eusebius hints at without any circumstantial details, took place in the Christian world. * * * He speaks also of the ambitious spirit of many, in aspiring to the offices of the Church, the ill-judged and unlawful ordinations, the quarrels among confessors themselves, and the contentions excited by young demagogues in the very relics of the persecuted Church, and the multiplied evils which their vices excited among Christians. How sadly must the Christian world have declined which could thus conduct itself under the very rod of divine vengeance? Yet let not the infidel or the profane world triumph. *It was not Christianity, but the departure from it,* which brought on these evils."[1]

14. The foregoing embodies but a few of the many evidences that could be cited in demonstration of the fact that during the period immediately following the apostolic ministry—the period covered by the persecutions of the Christians by the heathen nations,—the Church was undergoing internal deterioration, and was in a state of increasing perversion. Among the more detailed or specific cause of this ever widening departure from the spirit of the gospel of Christ, this rapidly growing apostasy, the following may be considered as important examples:

(1). The corrupting of the simple principles of the gospel by the admixture of the so-called philosophic systems of the times.

(2). Unauthorized additions to the ceremonies of the Church, and the introduction of vital changes in essential ordinances.

---

[1]Milner, "Church History," Cent. IV, ch. I. The Italics are introduced by the present writer. See also Note 5, end of chapter.

(3). Unauthorized changes in Church organization and government.

15. We shall consider in due order each of the three causes here enumerated. It may appear that the conditions set forth in these specifications are more properly to be regarded as effects or results, than as causes, incident to the general apostasy,—that they are in the nature of evidences or proofs of a departure from the original constitution of the Church, rather than specific causes by which the fact of apostasy is to be explained or accounted for. Cause and effect, however, are sometimes very intimately associated, and resulting conditions may furnish the best demonstration of causes in operation. Each of the conditions given above as a specific cause of the progressive apostasy was, at its inception, an evidence of existing unsoundness, and an active cause of the graver results that followed. Each succeeding manifestation of the spirit of apostasy was at once the result of earlier disaffection, and the cause of later and more pronounced developments.

Notes.

1. INORDINATE ZEAL MANIFESTED BY SOME OF THE EARLY CHRISTIANS: "The sober discretion of the present age will more readily censure than admire, but can more easily admire than imitate, the fervor of the first Christians; who, according to the lively expression of Sulpicius Severus, desired martyrdom with more eagerness than his own contemporaries solicited a bishopric. The epistles which Ignatius composed as he was carried in chains through the cities of Asia, breathe sentiments the most repugnant to the ordinary feelings of human nature. He earnestly beseeches the Romans that when he should be exposed in the amphitheatre, they would not by their kind but unreasonable intercession, deprive him of the crown of glory, and he declares his resolution to provoke and irritate the wild beasts which might be employed as the instruments of his death.

Some stories are related of the courage of martyrs who actually performed what Ignatius had intended: who exasperated the fury of the lions, pressed the executioner to hasten his office, cheerfully leaped into the fires which were kindled to consume them, and discovered a sensation of joy and pleasure in the midst of the most exquisite torture." (Gibbon, "Decline and Fall of the Roman Empire." ch. XVI.)

2. INTERNAL DISSENSIONS DURING TIME OF PEACE. As stated in the text the early part of Diocletian's reign—the period immediately preceding the outburst of the last great persecution to which the Christians were subjected—was a time of comparative freedom from opposition, and this period was characterized by internal disturbances and dissensions within the Church. Illustrative of the tolerance shown by the emperor before he became hostile to the Church, and the accompanying decline of spiritual earnestness among the Christians themselves, Gibbon says: "Diocletian and his colleagues frequently conferred the most important offices on those persons who avowed their abhorrence of the worship of the gods, but who had displayed abilities proper for the service of the state. The bishops held an honorable rank in the respective provinces, and were treated with distinction and respect, not only by the people, but by the magistrates themselves. Almost in every city the ancient churches were found insufficient to contain the increasing multitudes of proselytes; and in their place more stately and capacious edifices were erected for the public worship of the faithful. The corruption of manners and principles so forcibly lamented by Eusebius, may be considered not only as a consequence, but as a proof, of the liberty which the Christians enjoyed and abused under the reign of Diocletian. Prosperity had relaxed the nerves of discipline. Fraud, envy, and malice prevailed in every congregation. The presbyters aspired to the episcopal office, which every day became an object more worthy of their ambition. The bishops who contended with each other for ecclesiastical pre-eminence, appeared by their conduct to claim a secular and tyrannical power in the church; and the lively faith which still distinguished the Christians from the Gentiles, was shown much less in their lives than in their controversial writings." (Gibbon, "Decline and Fall of the Roman Empire," ch. XVI.)

3. THE EFFECT OF PEACE ON THE EARLY CHURCH. "Disastrous as the persecutions of the early Christian centuries were, still more

mischievous to the Church were those periods of tranquility which intervened between the outbursts of rage which prompted them. Peace may have her victories no less renowned than those of war; and so, too, she has her calamities, and they are not less destructive than those of war. War may destroy nations, but ease and luxury mankind corrupt — the body and the mind. Especially is peace dangerous to the church. Prosperity relaxes the reins of discipline; people feel less and less the need of a sustaining providence; but in adversity the spirit of man feels after God, and he is correspondingly more devoted to the service of religion. We shall find the early Christians no exception to the operation of this influence of repose. Whenever it was accorded them, either through the mercy or the indifference of the emperors, internal dissensions, the intrigues of aspiring prelates, and the rise of heresies, characterized those periods." (B. H. Roberts, "A New Witness for God," p. 70.)

4. SCHISMS AND HERESIES IN THE EARLY CHURCH. Eusebius, whose writings date from the early part of the fourth century, cites the writings of Hegesippus, who lived in the first quarter of the second century, as follows: "The same author [Hegesippus] also treats of the beginning of the heresies that arose about this time, in the following words: 'But after James the Just had suffered martyrdom, as our Lord had for the same reason, Simeon, the son of Cleophas, our Lord's uncle, was appointed the second bishop [of Jerusalem] whom all proposed as the cousin of our Lord. Hence they called the Church as yet a virgin, for it was not yet corrupted by vain discourses. Thebuthis made a beginning, secretly to corrupt it on account of his not being made bishop. He was one of those seven sects among the Jewish people. Of these also was Simeon, whence sprang the sect of Simonians; also Cleobius, from whence came the Cleobians; also Dositheus, the founder of the Dositheans. From these also sprung the Gortheonians, from Gorthoeus; and also Masbotheans from Masbothoeus. Hence also the Meandrians, and Marcionists, and Carpocratians and Valentinians, and Basilidians, and the Saturnillians, every one introducing his own peculiar opinions, one differing from the other. From these sprung the false Christs and the false prophets and false apostles, who divided the unity of the Church by the introduction of corrupt doctrines against God and against His Christ." (Eusebius, "Ecclesiastical History," Book IV, ch. 22.)

5. EARLY DECLINE OF THE CHURCH: Milner, summing up the conditions attending the Church at the end of the second century, says: "And here we close the view of the second century, which, for the most part exhibited proofs of divine grace, as strong, or nearly so, as the first. We have seen the same unshaken and simple faith of Jesus, the same love of God and of the brethren; and— that in which they singularly excelled modern Christians—the same heavenly spirit and victory over the world. But a dark shade is enveloping these divine glories. The Spirit of God is grieved already by the ambitious intrusions of self-righteous, argumentative refinements, and Pharisaic pride; and though it be more common to represent the most sensible decay of godliness as commencing a century later, to me it seems already begun." (Milner, "Church History," Cent. II, ch. 9.)

Mosheim, writing of conditions attending the closing years of the third century, says: "The ancient method of ecclesiastical government seemed in general still to subsist, while, at the same time, by imperceptible steps, it varied from the primitive rule and degenerated towards the form of a religious monarchy. * * * This change in the form of ecclesiastical government was soon followed by a train of vices, which dishonored the character and authority of those to whom the administration of the Church was committed. For, though several yet continued to exhibit to the world illustrative examples of primitive piety and Christian virtue, yet many were sunk in luxury and voluptuousness, puffed up with vanity, arrogance and ambition, possessed with a spirit of contention and discord, and addicted to many other vices that cast an undeserved reproach upon the holy religion of which they were the unworthy professors and ministers. This is testified in such an ample manner by the repeated complaints of many of the most respectable writers of this age, that truth will not permit us to spread the veil, which we should otherwise be desirous to cast over such enormities among an order so sacred. The bishops assumed in many places a princely authority, particularly those who had the greatest number of churches under their inspection, and who presided over the most opulent assemblies. They appropriated to their evangelical function the splendid ensigns of temporal majesty. A throne, surrounded with ministers, exalted above his equals the servant of the meek and humble Jesus; and sumptuous garments dazzled the eyes and the minds of the multitude into an ignorant veneration of their arrogated authority. The example of the bishops was ambitiously imitated by the presbyters, who, neglecting the sacred duties of their station, abandoned themselves to the indolence and delicacy of an effeminate and luxurious life. The deacons, beholding the presbyters deserting thus their functions, boldly usurped their rights and privileges, and the effects of a corrupt ambition were spread through every rank of the sacred order." (Mosheim, "Ecclesiastical History," Cent. III, Part II, ch. 2: 3, 4.)

.

CHAPTER VII.

1. First among the specific causes of disturbance operating within the Church, and contributing to its apostasy, we have named: *"The corrupting of simple principles of the gospel by the admixture of the so-called philosophic systems of the times."*

2. The attempted grafting of foreign doctrines on the true vine of the gospel of Christ was characteristic of the early years of the apostolic period. We read of the sorcerer Simon, who professed belief and entered the Church by baptism, but who was so devoid of the true spirit of the gospel that he sought to purchase by money the authority and power of the priesthood.[a] This man, though rebuked by Peter, and apparently penitent, continued to trouble the Church, by inculcating heresies and winning disciples within the fold. His followers were distinguished as a sect or cult down to the fourth century; and, writing at that time, Eusebius says of them: "These, after the manner of their founder, insinuating themselves into the Church, like a pestilential and leprous disease, infected those with the greatest corruption, into whom they were able to infuse their secret, irremediable, and destructive poison.[b] This Simon, known in history as Simon Magus, is referred to by early Christian writers as the founder of heresy, owing to his persistent attempts to combine Christianity with Gnosticism. It is with reference to his proposition to pur-

---

[a] See Acts 8: 9, 13, 18-24.
[b] Eusebius, "Ecclesiastical History," Book II, ch. 1.

chase spiritual authority that all traffic in spiritual offices has come to be known as simony.

3. Through the mouth of the Revelator, the Lord reproved certain of the churches for their adoption or toleration of doctrines and practices alien to the gospel. Notably is this the case with respect to the Nicolaitanes, and the followers of the doctrines of Balaam.[c]

4. The perversion of true theology thus developed within the Church is traceable to the introduction of both Judaistic and pagan fallacies.[d] Indeed, at the opening of the Christian era and for centuries thereafter, Judaism was more or less intimately mixed with pagan philosophy, and contaminated with heathen ceremonies. There were numerous sects and parties, cults and schools, each advocating rival theories as to the constitution of the soul, the essence of sin, the nature of Deity, and a multitude of other mysteries. The Christians were soon embroiled in endless controversies among themselves.

5. Judaistic converts to Christianity sought to modify and adapt the tenets of the new faith so as to harmonize them with their inherited love of Judaism, and the result was destructive to both. Our Lord had indicated the futility of any such attempt to combine new principles with old systems, or to patch up the prejudices of the past with fragments of new doctrine. "No man," said He, "putteth a piece of new cloth unto an old garment, for that which is put in to fill it up taketh from the garment, and the rent is made worse. Neither do men put new wine into old bot-

---

[c] See Rev. 2: 15; compare verse 6; see also verse 20. See Note 1, end of chapter.

[d] See Note 2, end of chapter.

tles; else the bottles break and the wine runneth out, and the bottles perish: but they put new wine into new bottles, and both are preserved."[e] The gospel came as a new revelation, marking the fulfilment of the law, it was no mere addendum, nor was it a simple re-enactment of past requirements; it embodied a new and an everlasting covenant. Attempts to patch the Judaistic robe with the new fabric of the gospel could result in nothing more sightly than a hideous rent. The new wine of the covenant could not be bottled in the time-eaten leathern containers of Mosaic libations. Judaism was belittled and Christianity perverted by the incongruous association.

6. Among the early and most pernicious adulterations of Christian doctrine is the introduction of the teachings of the Gnostics. These self-styled philosophers put forth the boastful claim that they were able to lead the human mind to a full comprehension of the Supreme Being, and a knowledge of the true relationship between Deity and mortals. They said in effect that a certain being had existed from all eternity, manifested as a radiant light diffused throughout space, and this they called the *Pleroma*. "The eternal nature, infinitely perfect and infinitely happy, having dwelt from everlasting in a profound solitude, and in a blessed tranquility, produced at length from itself, two minds of a different sex, which resembled their supreme parent in the most perfect manner. From the prolific union of these two beings, others arose, which were also followed by succeeding generations; so that in process of time a celestial family was formed in the Pleroma. This divine progeny, immutable in its nature, and above the power of mortality, was called, by the philosophers, *Aeon*—a term which signi-

---

*Matt. 9: 16, 17.

fies, in the Greek language, an eternal nature. How many in number these Aeons were was a point much controverted among the oriental sages."[1]

7. Then one of the Aeons, distinctively called the Demiurge, created this world, and arrogantly asserted dominion over the same, denying absolutely the authority of the supreme parent. The Gnostic doctrine declares man to be a union of a body, which, being the creation of the Demiurge, is essentially evil, and a spirit, which, being derived from Deity, is characteristically good. The spirits thus imprisoned in evil bodies will be finally liberated, and then the power of the Demiurge will cease, and the earth will be dissolved into nothingness.

8. Our justification for introducing here this partial summary of Gnosticism is the fact that early efforts were made to accommodate the tenets of this system to the demands of Christianity; and that Christ and the Holy Ghost were declared to belong to the family of Aeons provided for in this scheme. This led to the extravagant absurdity of denying that Jesus had a body even while He lived as a man; and that His appearance as a corporeal being was a deception of the senses wrought by His supernatural power.[2]

9. That the doctrines of the Gnostics were unsatisfying even to those who professed to believe therein is evident from the many cults and parties that came into existence as subdivisions of the main sect; and it is interesting to note that in modern times certain free-thinkers have prided themselves in assuming a title expressing the full antithesis of the name Gnostics, viz. Agnostics.

---

[1]Mosheim, "Ecclesiastical History," Cent. I, Part II, 1: 7.
[2]See Note 3, end of chapter.

10. The practical effect of the principles of Gnosticism in the lives of its adherents is strangely diverse. One division of the sect followed a life of austerity, embracing rigorous self-denial, and bodily torture, in the vain belief that the malignant body could thus be subdued, while the spirit would be given added power and increased freedom. Another cult sought to minimize the fundamental difference between right and wrong, by denying the element of morality in human life; and these abandoned themselves to the impulses of the passions and the frailties of the bodily nature without restraint, on the assumption that there was no such relation between body and soul as would cause injury to the latter through bodily indulgences and excesses.

11. Another sect or school whose doctrines were in a measure amalgamated with those of Christianity was that of the New Platonics. The ancient sects of Platonists or Platonics were allied in some points of doctrine with the Epicureans, and were rivals if not opponents of the Stoics. The early Platonics held that unorganized matter has existed from all eternity, and that its organizer, God, is similarly eternal. As God is eternal, so also His will or intelligence is without beginning, and this eternal intelligence existing as the will or intent of Deity, was called the *Logos*. Such precepts had been taught long before the Christian era, and the philosophy professed by some of the contending sects among the Jews in the time of Christ had been influenced thereby.

12. As the principles of Christianity became generally known, certain leaders in the sect of Platonics found in the new doctrine much to study and admire. By this time, however, Platonism itself had undergone much change, and the more liberal adherents had formed a new organization and

distinguished themselves by the appellation New Platonics. These professed to find in Jesus Christ the incarnation of the Logos, and accepted with avidity the declaration of St. John: "In the beginning was the Word, and the Word was with God, and the Word was God. * * * * * And the Word was made flesh and dwelt among us."[h] According to the Eclectic or New Platonic philosophy, the "Word" referred to by St. John was the "Logos" described by Plato.

13. The Platonic conception of the Godhead as consisting of the Deity and the Logos, was enlarged in accordance with Christian tenets to embrace three members, the Holy Ghost being the third. Thence arose bitter and lasting dissension as to the relative powers of each member of the Trinity, particularly the position and authority of the Logos or Son. The many disputes incident to the admixture of Platonic theory with Christian doctrine continued through the centuries, and in a sense may be said to trouble the minds of men even in this modern age.

14. It is wholly beyond our purpose to classify or describe the hybrid offspring resulting from the unnatural union of pagan philosophy and Christian truth; nor shall we attempt to follow in detail the dissensions and quarrels on theological points and questions of doctrine. Our purpose is achieved when by statement of fact and citation of authority, the reality of the apostasy is established. We shall consider therefore only the most important of the dissensions by which the Church was troubled.[i]

15. About the middle of the third century, Sibellius, a presbyter or bishop of the church in Africa, strongly advo-

---

[h]John 1: 1, 14.
[i]See Note 4, end of chapter.

cated the doctrine of "trinity in unity" as characterizing the Godhead. He claimed that the divine nature of Christ was no distinct nor personal attribute of the man Jesus, but merely a portion of the divine energy, an emanation from the Father, with which the Son was temporarily endowed; and that in like manner the Holy Ghost was a part of the divine Father. These views were as vigorously opposed by some as defended by others, and the disagreement was rife when Constantine so suddenly changed the status of the Church, and brought to its support the power of the state. Early in the fourth century the dispute assumed a threatening aspect in a bitter contention between Alexander, bishop of Alexandria, and Arius, one of the subordinate officers of the same church. Alexander prcolaimed that the Son was in all respects the equal of the Father, and also of the same substance or essence. Arius insisted that the Son had been created by the Father, and therefore could not be co-eternal with His divine Parent; that the Son was the agent through whom the will of the Father was executed, and that for this reason also the Son was inferior to the Father both in nature and dignity. In like manner the Holy Ghost was inferior to the other members of the Godhead.

16. Arianism, as the doctrine came to be known, was preached with vigor and denounced with energy; and the dissension thus occasioned threatened to rend the Church to its foundation. At last the emperor, Constantine, was forced to intervene in an effort to establish peace among his contending churchmen. He summoned a council of church dignitaries which assembled in the year 325, and which is known from its place of session as the Council of Nice. This council condemned the doctrine of Arius, and pronounced sentence of banishment against its author. What was declared to be the orthodox doctrine of the

universal or Catholic church respecting the Godhead was promulgated as follows:

17. "We believe in one God, the Father, Almighty, the maker of all things visible and invisible; and in one Lord, Jesus Christ, the Son of God, begotten of the Father, only begotten, (that is) of the substance of the Father; God of God, Light of Light; Very God of Very God; begotten not made; of the same substance with the Father, by whom all things were made, that are in heaven and that are in earth: who for us men, and for our salvation, descended and was incarnate, and became man; suffered and rose again the third day, ascended into the heavens and will come to judge the living and the dead; and in the Holy Spirit. But those who say there was a time when he [the Son] was not, and that he was not before he was begotten, and that he was made out of nothing, or affirm that he is of any other substance or essence, or that the Son of God was created, and mutable, or changeable, the Catholic Church doth pronounce accursed."

18. This is the generally accepted version of the Nicene Creed as originally promulgated. In form it was somewhat modified, though left practically unchanged as to essentials, by the council held at Constantinople half a century later. What is regarded as a restatement of the Nicene Creed has been attributed to Athanasius, one of the chief opponents of Arianism, though his right to be considered the author is questioned by many and emphatically denied by some authorities on ecclesiastical history. Nevertheless, the statement referred to has found a place in literature as the "Creed of Athanasius," and whether rightly or wrongly named it persists as a declaration of belief professed by some Christian sects today. It has a present place in the pre-

scribed ritual of the Church of England. The "Creed of Athanasius" reads as follows:

19. "We worship one God in Trinity, and Trinity in Unity, neither confounding the persons, nor dividing the substance. For there is one person of the Father, another of the Son, and another of the Holy Ghost. But the Godhead of the Father, Son, and Holy Ghost, is all one: the glory equal, the majesty co-eternal. Such as the Father is, such is the Son; and such is the Holy Ghost. The Father uncreate, the Son uncreate, and the Holy Ghost uncreate. The Father incomprehensible, the Son incomprehensible and the Holy Ghost incomprehensible. The Father eternal, the Son eternal, and the Holy Ghost eternal. And yet there are not three eternals; but one eternal. As also there are not three incomprehensibles, nor three uncreated; but one uncreated, and one incomprehensible. So likewise the Father is Almighty, the Son Almighty, and the Holy Ghost Almighty; and yet there are not three Almighties, but one Almighty. So the Father is God, the Son is God, and the Holy Ghost is God, and yet they are not three Gods but one God."

20. The Council of Nice is known in ecclesiastical history as one of the most famous and important gatherings ever assembled as an official body concerned with church administration. Not only was the Arian dispute disposed of, so far as ecclesiastical decree could dispose of a question vitally affecting the individual conscience, but many other subjects of controversy were similarly quieted for the time. Thus the long-standing dispute as to the time of celebrating Easter was settled by vote, as was also the question agitated by Novatus and his followers—as to the propriety of re-admitting repentant apostates to the Church; and the schism caused by Meletius, a bishop of Upper

Africa, who had refused to recognize the superior authority of the bishop of Alexandria. From the number and diversity of the questions brought before the Nicene Council for adjudication, we may safely conclude that the newly enthroned Church was not characterized by unity of purpose nor harmony of action. However, compared with the bitter contentions that follow, the dissensions in the reign of Constantine were but as the beginnings of trouble.

21. The moral effect of the potent spirit of apostasy operating through the first three centuries of the Church's existence and nourished by the contributions of heathen philosophy, proved, as was inevitable, highly injurious and evil. Some of the most pernicious of these effects it becomes our duty to consider.

22. *Perverted view of life.* One of the heresies of early origin and rapid growth in the Church was the doctrine of antagonism between body and spirit, whereby the former was regarded as an incubus and a curse. From what has been said this will be recognized as one of the perversions derived from the alliance of Gnosticism with Christianity. A result of this grafting in of heathen doctrines was an abundant growth of hermit practices, by which men sought to weaken, torture, and subdue their bodies, that their spirits or "souls" might gain greater freedom. Many who adopted this unnatural view of human existence retired to the solitude of the desert, and there spent their time in practices of stern self-denial and in acts of frenzied self-torture. Others shut themselves up as voluntary prisoners, seeking glory in privation and self-imposed penance. It was this unnatural view of life that gave rise to the several orders of recluses, hermits, and monks.

23. Think you not that the Savior had such practices in mind, when, warning the disciples of the false claims to sanctity that would characterize the times then soon to follow, He said: "Wherefore if they shall say unto you, Behold he [Christ] is in the desert, go not forth: behold, he is in the secret chambers, believe it not."[j]

24. When the Church came into the favor of the state under Constantine in the fourth century, there sprang up many orders of recluses who "maintained that communion with God was to be sought by mortifying sense, by withdrawing the mind from all external objects, by macerating the body with hunger and labor, and by a holy sort of indolence, which confined all the activity of the soul to a lazy contemplation of things spiritual and external." Mosheim, the author just quoted, continues: "The Christian church would never have been disgraced by this cruel and unsocial enthusiasm, nor would any have been subjected to those keen torments of mind and body to which it gave rise, had not many Christians been unwarily caught by the specious appearance and the pompous sound of that maxim of the ancient philosophy: 'That in order to the attainment of true felicity and communion with God, it was necessary that the soul should be separated from the body, even here below; and that the body was to be macerated and mortified for this purpose.' "[k]

25. The fruit of this ill-sowing was the growth of numerous orders of monks, and the maintenance of monasteries. Celibacy was taught as a virtue, and came to be made a requirement of the clergy, as it is in the Roman Catholic church today. An unmarried clergy, deprived of the elevating influences of home life, fell into many ex-

---

[j]Matt. 24: 26.
[k]Mosheim, "Eccl. Hist," Cent. IV, Part II, ch. 3: 12, 13.

cesses, and the corruption of the priests has been a theme of
reproach throughout the centuries. "The Lord God said,
It is not good that the man should be alone; I will make him
an help-meet for him,"[l] and again "Therefore shall a man
leave his father and his mother, and shall cleave unto his
wife; and they shall be one flesh."[m] His inspired apostle
proclaimed: "Neither is the man without the woman, neither
the woman without the man, in the Lord."[n] Nevertheless
an apostate church decrees that its ministers shall be forbidden to follow the law of God.

26. *Disregard for truth.* As early as the fourth century,
certain pernicious doctrines embodying a disregard for
truth gained currency in the Church. Thus, it was taught
"that it was an act of virtue to deceive and lie, when by
that means the interests of the church might be promoted."[o]
Needless to say, sins other than those of falsehood and deceit were justified when committed in the supposed interests of church advancement, and crime was condoned under
the specious excuse that the end justifies the means. Many
of the fables and fictitious stories relating to the lives of
Christ and the apostles, as also the spurious accounts of supernatural visitations and wonderful miracles, in which the
literature of the early centuries abound, are traceable to
this infamous doctrine that lies are acceptable unto God if
perpetrated in a cause that man calls good.[p]

Notes.

1. THE NICOLAITANES. This sect is mentioned specifically in the
divine communication wherein John the Revelator was instructed

[l]Gen. 2: 18.
[m]Verse 24.
[n]I Cor. 11: 11. Compare I Tim. IV, 3.
[o]Mosheim, "Eccl. Hist.," Cent. IV, Part II, ch. 3:16.
[p]See Note 5, end of chapter.

to write to the churches of Asia (Rev. 2: 6, 15); and the reference proves the abhorrence with which the Lord regarded the teachings and practices of the cult. The attempt to corrupt Christianity by the introduction of Nicolaitan ceremonies was a real danger threatening the Church. The following extract from Smith's Bible Dictionary is instructive:

"The sect itself comes before us as presenting the ultimate phase of a great controversy, which threatened at one time to destroy the unity of the Church, and afterward to taint its purity. The controversy itself was inevitable as soon as the Gentiles were admitted in any large numbers into the Church of Christ. Were the new converts to be brought into subjugation to the whole Mosaic law? The apostles and elders at Jerusalem met the question calmly and wisely. The burden of the Law was not to be imposed on the Gentile disciples. They were to abstain, among other things, from 'meats offered to idols,' and from 'fornication' (Acts 15: 20, 29), and this decree was welcomed as the great charter of the Church's freedom. Strange as the close union of the moral and the positive commands may seem to us, it did not seem so to the synod at Jerusalem. The two sins were very closely allied, often even in the closest proximity of time and place. The messages to the churches of Asia, and the later Apostolic Epistles (II Peter, and Jude) indicate that the two evils appeared at that period also in close alliance. The teachers of the Church branded them with a name that expressed their true character. Then men who did and taught such things were followers of Balaam (II Peter 2: 15; Jude 11.) They, like the false prophet of Pethor, united brave words with evil deeds. In a time of persecution, when the eating or not eating of things sacrificed to idols was more than ever a crucial test of faithfulness, they persuaded men more than ever that it was a thing indifferent (Rev. 2: 13, 14). This was bad enough, but there was a yet worse evil. Mingling themselves in the orgies of idolatrous feasts, they brought the impurities of those feasts into the meetings of the Christian Church. And all this was done, it must be remembered, not simply as an indulgence of appetite, but as part of a system supported by a 'doctrine,' accompanied by the boast of a prophetic illumination (II Peter 2: 1)."

2. IMITATION OF HEATHEN MYSTERIES, AND THE RESULT. The worship of God by the early Christians was decried and ridiculed because of its simplicity and the absence of mystic ceremonies. True, the zeal of persecutors soon made necessary a prudent secrecy in religious service and worshiping assemblies, but, aside from such necessity, there was a voluntary effort to feign a secrecy that was uncalled for. On this point Gibbon remarks as follows: "The precautions with which the disciples of Christ performed the offices of religion were at first dictated by fear and necessity; but they were continued from choice. By imitating the awful secrecy of the Eleusinian mysteries, the Christians had flattered themselves that they should render their sacred institutions more respectable in the eyes of the pagan world. But the event, as it often happens to the operations of subtle policy, deceived their wishes and their expectations. It was concluded that they only concealed what they would have blushed to disclose. Their mistaken prudence afforded an opportunity for malice to invent, and for suspicious credulity to believe, the horrid tales which described the Christians as the most wicked of human kind, who practiced in their dark recesses every abomination that a depraved fancy could suggest, and who solicited the favor of their unknown God by the sacrifice of every moral virtue. There were many who pretended to confess or to relate the ceremonies of this abhorred society." (Gibbon, "Decline and Fall of the Roman Empire," chap. XVI.)

3. EBIONITES AND GNOSTICS. "Beside the general design of fixing on a perpetual basis the divine honors of Christ, the most ancient and respectable of the ecclesiastical writers have ascribed to the evangelic theologian [St. John] a particular intention to confute two opposing heresies, which disturbed the peace of the primitive Church. I. The faith of the Ebionites, perhaps of the Nazarenes, was gross and imperfect. They revered Jesus as the greatest of the prophets, endowed with supernatural virtue and power. They ascribed to his person and to his future reign all the predictions of the Hebrew oracles which relate to the spiritual and everlasting kingdom of the promised Messiah. Some of them might confess that He was born of a virgin; but they obstinately rejected the preceding existence and divine perfections of the Logos, or Son of God, which are so clearly

defined in the Gospel of St. John. ° ° ° II. The Gnostics, who were distinguished by the epithet of Docetes, deviated into the contrary extreme, and betrayed the human while they asserted the divine, nature of Christ. Educated in the school of Plato, accustomed to the sublime idea of the Logos, they readily conceived that the brightest Aeon or Emanation of the Deity, might assume the outward shape and visible appearance of a mortal; but they vainly pretended that the imperfections of matter are incompatible with the purity of a celestial substance. While the blood of Christ yet smoked on Mount Calvary, the Docetes invented the impious and extravagant hypothesis that, instead of issuing from the womb of the Virgin, he had descended on the banks of the Jordan in the form of perfect manhood; that he had imposed on the senses of His enemies and of His disciples, and that the ministers of Pilate had wasted their impotent rage on an airy phantom, who seemed to expire on the cross, and, after three days, to rise from the dead" (Gibbon, "Decline and Fall of the Roman Empire," ch. XXI.)

4. ADMIXTURE OF PAGAN DOCTRINES WITH CHRISTIANITY. The following statements by modern writers as to the effect of pagan "philosophy" on the Church are worthy of attention. Summarizing conditions prevailing in the latter part of the second century, Milner says: "We have hitherto found it no hard matter to discover, in the teachers and writers of Christianity, the vital doctrines of Christ. We shall now perceive that the most precious truths of the gospel begin to be less attended to, and less brought to view. Even Justin Martyr, before the period of eclectic corruption, by his fondness for Plato, adulterated the gospel in some degree, as we have observed particularly in the article of free will. Tatian, his scholar, went bolder lengths, and deserved the name of heretic. He dealt largely in the merits of continence and chastity; and these virtues, pushed into extravagant excesses, under the notion of superior purity, became great engines of self-righteousness and superstition; obscured men's views of the faith of Christ, and darkened the whole face of Christianity. Under the fostering hand of Ammonius and his followers, this fictitious holiness disguised under the appearance of eminent sanctity, was formed into a system; and it soon began to generate the worst of evils. ° ° ° St. Paul's caution against philosophy and vain deceit, it appears, was now fatally neglected by the Christians. False humil-

ity, 'will-worship," curious and proud refinements, bodily austerities mixed with high, self-righteous pretensions, ignorance of Christ and of the true life of faith in Him, miserably superseded by ceremonies and superstitions,—all these things are divinely delineated in the second chapter to the Colossians; and, so far as words can do it, the true defense against them is powerfully described and enforced." (Milner, "Church History," Cent. II, ch. 9.)

"The schisms and commotions that arose in the church, from a mixture of the oriental and Egyptian philosophy with the Christian religion were, in the second century, increased by those Grecian philosophers who embraced the doctrine of Christ. The Christian doctrine, concerning the Father, Son, and Holy Ghost, and the two natures united in our blessed Savior, were by no means reconcilable with the tenets of the sages and doctors of Greece, who therefore endeavored to explain them in such a manner as to render them comprehensible. Praxeas, a man of genius and learning, began to propagate these explications at Rome, and was severely persecuted for the errors they contained. He denied any real distinction between the Father, Son, and Holy Ghost; and maintained that the Father, sole Creator of all things, had united to himself the human nature of Christ. Hence his followers were called Monarchians, because of their denying a plurality of persons in the Deity; and also Patropassians, because, according to Tertullian's account, they believed that the Father was so intimately united with the man Christ, his Son, that he suffered with him the anguish of an afflicted life and the torments of an ignominious death. However ready many may have been to embrace this erroneous doctrine, it does not appear that this sect formed to themselves a separate place of worship, or removed themselves from the ordinary assemblies of Christians." (Mosheim, "Ecclesiastical History," Cent. II, Part II, ch. 5: 20.)

5. SPURIOUS WRITINGS IN THE APOSTOLIC PERIOD. "Not long after Christ's ascension into heaven, several histories of his life and doctrines, full of pious frauds and fabulous wonders, were composed by persons whose intentions, perhaps, were not bad, but whose writings discovered the greatest superstition and ignorance. Nor was this all: productions appeared which were imposed upon the world by fraudulent men, as the writings of the holy apostles. These apoc-

ryphal and spurious writings must have produced a sad confusion, and rendered both the history and the doctrine of Christ uncertain, had not the rulers of the church used all possible care and diligence in separating the books that were truly apostolical and divine from all that spurious trash." (Mosheim, "Ecclesiastical History," Cent. I, Part II, ch. 2: 17.)

CHAPTER VIII.

1. As one of the effective causes leading to the apostasy of the Primitive Church we have specified: *Unauthorized additions to the ceremonies of the Church, and the introduction of vital changes in essential ordinances.*

2. The ridicule heaped upon the early Church by the pagans on account of the simplicity of Christian worship has already received mention. This cause of reproach was none the less emphasized by Judaistic critics, to whom ritual and ceremony, formalism and prescribed rites, figured as essentials of religion. Very early in its history, the Church manifested a tendency to supplant the pristine simplicity of its worship by elaborate ceremonies, patterned after Judaistic ritual and heathen idolatries.

3. As to such innovations, Mosheim writes as follows, with reference to conditions existing in the second century: "There is no institution so pure and excellent which the corruption and folly of man will not in time alter for the worse, and load with additions foreign to its nature and original design. Such in a particular manner was the fate of Christianity. In this century many unnecessary rites and ceremonies were added to the Christian worship, the introduction of which was extremely offensive to wise and good men. These changes, while they destroyed the beautiful simplicity of the gospel, were naturally pleasing to the gross multitude, who are more delighted with the pomp and splendor of external institutions than with the native charms of rational and solid piety, and who generally give

little attention to any objects but those which strike their outward senses."[a] The author just cited explains that the bishops of that day increased the ceremonies and sought to give them splendor "by way of accommodation to the infirmities and prejudices of both Jews and heathen."[b]

4. To more effectually reconcile the gospel requirements with Jewish prejudice, which still clung to the letter of the Mosaic law, the officers of the Church in the first and second centuries took to themselves the ancient titles; thus, bishops styled themselves chief priests, and deacons, Levites. "In like manner," says Mosheim, "the comparison of the Christian *oblation* with the Jewish *victim* and *sacrifice,* produced a multitude of unnecessary rites, and was the occasion of introducing that erroneous notion of the *eucharist,* which represents it as real sacrifice, and not merely as a commemoration of that great offering that was once made upon the cross for the sins of mortals."[c]

5. In the fourth century we find the Church still more hopelessly committed to formalism and superstition. The decent respect with which the remains of the early martyrs had been honored degenerated or grew into a superstitious reverence amounting to worship. This practice was allowed in deference to the heathen adoration paid to deified heroes. Pilgrimages to the tombs of martyrs became common as an outward form of religious devotion; and the ashes of martyrs as well as dust and earth brought from places said to have been made holy by some uncommon occurrences were sold as sovereign remedies against disease and as means of protection against the assaults of malignant spirits.

---

[a] Mosheim, "Eccl. Hist.," Cent. II, Part II, ch. 4.
[b] See Note 1, end of chapter.
[c] Mosheim, "Eccl. Hist.," Cent. II, Part II, ch. 4: 4.

6. The form of public worship was so changed during the second and third centuries as to bear little resemblance to the simplicity and earnestness of that of the early congregations. Philosophic discourses took the place of fervent testimony bearing, and the arts of the rhetorician and controversial debater supplanted the true eloquence of religious conviction. Applause was allowed and expected as evidence of the preacher's popularity. The burning of incense, at first abhorred by Christian assemblies because of its pagan origin and heathen significance, had become common in the Church before the end of the third century.

7. In the fourth century the adoration of images, pictures, and effigies, had been given a place in the so-called Christian worship; and the practice became general in the century following. An effort to check the abuses arising from this idolatrous practice in the eighth century, actually led to civil war.[d]

8. In considering such evidences of pagan ceremonial and superstitious rites taking the place of the simple procedure incident to genuine worship characteristic of the Church in the days of its integrity, who can question the solemn and awful fact of actual apostasy?[e] But more important yet, more significant still than mere additions to the ritualistic ceremonial, are the perversions and changes introduced into the most sacred and essential ordinances of Christ's Church. As it is common with ecclesiastical authorities to consider the most essential ordinances of the gospel originally established by Christ and maintained by His apostles, as comprising baptism and the sacrament of the Lord's supper, we shall examine into these alone as exam-

[d]See Mosheim, "Eccl. Hist.," Cent. VIII, Part II, ch. 3: **9, 10.**
[e]See Note 2, end of chapter.

ples of the unauthorized alterations now under consideration. In this restriction of our illustrative examples we do not admit that baptism and the sacrament named were the only ordinances characterizing the Church; indeed, there is abundant proof to the contrary. Thus, the authoritative imposition of hands for the bestowal of the Holy Ghost in the case of baptized believers was equally essential with baptism itself,[f] and was assuredly regarded as a vital ordinance from the first.[g] Furthermore, ordination in the priesthood, whereby men were commissioned by divine authority, was indispensable to the maintenance of an organized Church. The examples selected, however, will be sufficient for the purposes of our present inquiry.

THE ORDINANCE OF BAPTISM CHANGED.

9.   First, then, as to baptism,—in what did the ordinance originally consist, as to purpose and mode of administration, and what changes did it undergo in the course of progressive apostasy through which the Church passed? That baptism is essential to salvation calls for no demonstration here; this has been generally held by the Christian Church in both ancient and modern times.[h] The purpose of baptism was and is the obtaining of a remission of sins; compliance with the requirement has been from the first the sole means of securing admission to the Church of Christ.[i]

---

[f]See Acts 8: 5-8, 12, 14-17; also 19: 1-7; see also 2: 38; Matt. 3: 11; and Mark 1: 8.

[g]See Matt. 3: 11.

[h]For a concise treatment of this subject see the author's "Articles of Faith," Lecture 6: 8-29.

[i]See Mark 1: 4 and Luke 3: 3; also Acts 2: 38; I Peter 3: 21; and Acts 22: 16. Compare II Nephi, 31: 17.

10. In the early Church, baptism was administered on profession of faith and evidence of repentance, and was performed by immersion[j] at the hands of one invested with the requisite authority of priesthood. There was no delay in administering the ordinance after the eligibility of the candidate had been shown. As instances we may cite the promptness with which baptism was administered to the believers on that eventful day of Pentecost;[k] the baptism administered by Philip to the Ethiopian convert immediately following due profession of faith;[l] the undelayed baptism of devout Cornelius and his family;[m] and the speedy baptism of the converted jailor by Paul, his prisoner.[n]

11. In the second century, however, priestly mandate had restricted the baptismal ordinance to the times of the two Church festivals, Easter and Whitsuntide, the first being the anniversary of Christ's resurrection, and the second the time of Pentecostal celebration. A long and tedious course of preparation was required of the candidate before his eligibility was admitted; during this time he was known as a *catechumen,* or novice in training. According to some authorities a three years' course of preparation was required in all but exceptional cases.[o]

12. During the second century the baptismal symbolism of a new birth was emphasized by many additions to the ordinance; thus the newly baptized were treated as infants and were fed milk and honey in token of their immaturity. As baptism was construed to be a ceremony of liberation

---

[j]See Note 3, end of chapter.
[k]Acts 2: 37-41.
[l]Acts 8: 26-39.
[m]Acts 10: 47, 48.
[n]Acts 16: 31-33.
[o]Schlegel, Book VIII, ch. 32.

from the slavery of Satan, certain formulas used in the freeing of slaves were added. Anointing with oil was also made a part of the ceremony. In the third century the simple ordinance of baptism was further encumbered and perverted by the ministrations of an exorcist. This official indulged in "menacing and formidable shouts and declamation" whereby the demons or evil spirits with which the candidate was supposed to be afflicted were to be driven away. "The driving out this demon was now considered as an essential preparation for baptism, after the administration of which the candidates returned home, adorned with crowns, and arrayed in white garments, as sacred emblems, —the former of their victory over sin and the world; the latter of their inward purity and innocence."[p] It is not difficult to see in this superstitious ceremony the evidence of pagan adulteration of the Christian religion. In the fourth century it became the practice to place salt in the mouth of the newly baptized member, as a symbol of purification, and the actual baptism was both preceded and followed by an anointing with oil.

13. The form or mode of baptism also underwent a radical change during the first half of the third century,— a change whereby its essential symbolism was destroyed. Immersion,[q] typifying death followed by resurrection, was no longer deemed an essential feature, and sprinkling with water was allowed in place thereof. No less an authority than Cyprian, the learned bishop of Carthage, advocated the propriety of sprinkling in lieu of immersion in cases of physical weakness; and the practice thus started, later became general. The first instance of record is that of Novatus,

---

[p]Mosheim, "Eccl. Hist.," Cent. III, Part II, ch. 4: 4.

[q]See Note 3, end of chapter.

a heretic who requested baptism when he thought death was near.[r]

14.   Not only was the form of the baptismal rite radically changed, but the application of the ordinance was perverted. The practice of administering baptism to infants was recognized as orthodox in the third century and was doubtless of earlier origin. In a prolonged disputation as to whether it was safe to postpone the baptism of infants until the eighth day after birth—in deference to the Jewish custom of performing circumcision on that day—it was generally decided that such delay would be dangerous, as jeopardizing the future well-being of the child should it die before attaining the age of eight days, and that baptism ought to be administered as soon after birth as possible.[s] A more infamous doctrine than that of the condemnation of un-baptized infants can scarcely be imagined, and a stronger proof of the heresies that had invaded and corrupted the early Church need not be sought. Such a doctrine is foreign to the gospel and to the Church of Christ, and its adoption as an essential tenet is proof of apostasy.[t]

CHANGES IN THE ORDINANCE OF THE SACRAMENT OF THE LORD'S SUPPER

15.   The sacrament of the Lord's Supper has been regarded as an essential ordinance from the time of its establishment in the Church of Jesus Christ. Yet in spite of its sanctity it has undergone radical alteration both as to its

---

[r]As to the scriptural doctrine of baptism, the mode of its administration and the symbolism thereof, see the author's "Articles of Faith," Lecture 7.

[s]See Milner, "Church History," Cent. III; ch. 13.

[t]For a discussion of infant baptism, see the author's "Articles of Faith," Lecture 6. See Note 4, end of chapter.

symbolism and its accepted purpose. The sacrament, as insituted by the Savior and as administered during the days of the apostolic ministry, was as simple as it was sacred and solemn. Accompanied by the true spirit of the gospel its simplicity was sanctifying; as interpreted by the spirit of apostasy its simplicity became a reproach. Hence we find that in the third century, long sacramental prayers were prescribed, and much pomp was introduced. Vessels of gold and silver were used by such congregations as could afford them, and this with ostentatious display. Non-members and members "who were in a penitential state" were excluded from the sacramental service—in imitation of the exclusiveness accompanying heathen mysteries. Disputation and dissension arose as to the proper time of administering the sacrament—morning, noon, or evening; and as to the frequency with which the ordinance should be celebrated.[u]

16. At a later date the doctrine of *Transubstantiation* was established as an essential tenet of the Roman Church. This briefly summarized, is to the effect that the species, i. e., the bread and wine used in the sacrament, lose their character as mere bread and wine, and become in fact the flesh and blood of the crucified Christ. The transmutation is assumed to take place in such a mystical way as to delude the sense; and so, though actual flesh and actual blood, the elements still appear to be bread and wine. This view, so strongly defended and earnestly reverenced by orthodox members of the Roman Church, is vehemently denounced by others as "an absurd tenet,"[v] and a "monstrous and unnatural doctrine."[w]

---

[u]See Note 5, end of chapter.
[v]Milner.
[w]Mosheim.

17. There has been much discussion as to the origin of this doctrine,[z] the Roman Catholics claiming for it a great antiquity, while their opponents insist that it was an innovation of the eighth or ninth century. According to Milner it was openly taught in the ninth century;[y] was formally established as a dogma of the Church by the Council of Placentia A. D. 1095,[z] and was made an essential article of creed, belief in which was required of all, by action of the Roman ecclesiastical court about 1160.[a] An official edict of the pope, Innocent III, confirmed the dogma as a binding tenet and requirement of the Church in 1215;[b] and it remains practically in force in the Roman Catholic Church today. The doctrine was adopted by the Greek Church in the seventeenth century.[c]

18. The consecrated emblems, or "host," being regarded as the actual flesh and blood of Christ, were adored as of themselves divine. Thus, "a very pernicious practice of idolatry was connected with the reception of this doctrine. Men fell down before the consecrated host, and worshiped it as God; and the novelty, absurdity, and impiety of this abomination very much struck the minds of all men who were not dead to a sense of true religion."[d] The "elevation of the host," i. e., the presentation of the consecrated emblems before the congregation for adoration, is a feature of the present day ritual of worship in the Roman Catholic Church. The celebration of the mass is taught to be an actual though mystic sacrifice, in which the Son of God is

[z]See Note 6, end of chapter.
[y]Milner, "Church History," Cent. IX, ch. I.
[z]The same, Cent. XIII, ch. 1.
[b]Mosheim, "Eccl. Hist.," Cent. XIII, Part II, ch. 3: 2.
[c]The same, Cent. XVII, Part II, ch. 2: 3.
[d]Milner, "Church History," Cent. XIII, ch. I.

daily offered up anew as a constantly recurring atonement
for the present sins of the assembled worshipers. A further
perversion of the sacrament occurred in the administration
of bread alone, instead of both bread and wine as originally
required.

19. Thus was the plain purpose and assured efficacy of
the sacrament hidden beneath a cloud of mystery and ceremonial display. Contrast such with the solemn simplicity
of the ordinance as instituted by our Lord, — He took
bread and wine, blessed them and gave to His disciples
and said, "This do in remembrance of me."[e] Of the bread
He said, "This is my body;" of the wine, "This is my
blood;" yet at that time His body was unpierced, His blood
was unshed. The disciples ate bread, not flesh of a living
man, and drank wine, not blood; and this they were commanded to do in remembrance of Christ.[f] The perversion
of the sacrament is evidence of departure from the spirit
of the gospel of Christ, and when made an essential dogma
of a church is proof of the apostate condition of that church.

20. Behold, *"they have transgressed the laws, changed
the ordinance, broken the everlasting covenant."*[g]

Notes.

1. CEREMONIES ADDED AS A COMPROMISE. "Both Jews and heathens were accustomed to a vast variety of pompous and magnificent
ceremonies in their religious service. And as they considered these

------

[e]Luke 22: 19, 20, compare Matt. 26: 27, 28.

[f]For a general treatment of the Sacrament of the Lord's Supper, see
the author's "Articles of Faith," Lecture 9.

[g]See Isaiah 24: 4-6.

rites as an essential part of religion, it was but natural that they should behold with indifference, and even with contempt, the simplicity of the Christian worship, which was destitute of those idle ceremonies that rendered their service so specious and striking. To remove then, in some measure, this prejudice against Christianity, the bishops thought it necessary to increase the number of rites and ceremonies, and thus to render the public worship more striking to the outward senses. This addition of external rites was also designed to remove the opprobrious calumnies which the Jewish and pagan priests cast upon the Christians on account of the simplicity of their worship, esteeming them little better than atheists, because they had no temples, altars, victims, priests, nor anything of that external pomp in which the vulgar are so prone to place the essence of religion. The rulers of the Church adopted, therefore, certain external ceremonies, that thus they might captivate the senses of the vulgar, and be able to refute the reproaches of their adversaries." (Mosheim, "Ecclesiastical History," Cent. II, Part II, Ch. 4: 2, 3.)

A note appended to the foregoing excerpt by the translator, Dr. Archibald Maclaine, reads as follows:

"A remarkable passage in the life of Gregory, surnamed Thaumaturgus, i. e., the wonder worker, will illustrate this point in the clearest manner. The passage is as follows: 'When Gregory perceived that the ignorant multitude persisted in their idolatry, on account of the pleasures and sensual gratifications which they enjoyed at the pagan festivals, he granted them a permission to indulge themselves in the like pleasures, in celebrating the memory of the holy martyrs, hoping that in process of time, they would return of their own accord to a more virtuous and regular course of life.' There is no sort of doubt, but that by this permission, Gregory allowed the Christians to dance, sport, and feast at the tombs of the martyrs upon their respective festivals, and to do everything which the pagans were accustomed to do in their temples during the feasts celebrated in honor of their gods."

The Gregory referred to in the note last quoted flourished about the middle of the third century. He acquired the title Thaumaturgus from his fame as a worker of miracles, the genuineness of which achievements is disputed by many authorities. He was bishop of

New Caesarea, and a man of great influence in the Church. His
sanction of ceremonies, patterned after pagan rites, was doubtless of
far-reaching effect.

2. CHURCH CEREMONIAL IN THE FIFTH CENTURY. "The sublime
and simple theology of the primitive Christians was gradually corrupted, and the Monarchy of heaven, already clouded by meta-
physical subtleties, was degraded by the introduction of a popular
mythology, which tended to restore the reign of polytheism. As
the objects of religion were gradually reduced to the standard of
the imagination, the rites and ceremonies were introduced that
seemed most powerfully to affect the senses of the vulgar. If, in the
beginning of the fifth century, Tertullian or Lactantius had been
suddenly raised from the dead, to assist at the festival of some popular saint or martyr, they would have gazed with astonishment and
indignation on the profane spectacle, which had succeeded to the
pure and spiritual worship of a Christian congregation. As soon as
the doors of the Church were thrown open they must have been
offended by the smoke of incense, the perfume of flowers, and the
glare of lamps and tapers, which diffused, at noonday, a gaudy, super-
fluous, and, in their opinion a sacrilegious light. If they approached
the balustrade of the altar, they made their way through the prostrate
crowd, consisting for the most part, of strangers and pilgrims, who
resorted to the city on the vigil of the feast; and who already felt
the strong intoxication of fanaticism, and perhaps of wine. Their
devout kisses were imprinted on the walls and pavements of the
sacred edifice; and their fervent prayers were directed, whatever
might be the language of their church, to the bones, the blood, or the
ashes of the saints, which were usually concealed by a linen or silken
veil from the eyes of the vulgar. The Christians frequented the tombs
of the martyrs, in the hope of obtaining, from their powerful intercession, every sort of spiritual, but more especially of temporal blessings. * * * The same uniform original spirit of superstition might
suggest, in the most distant ages and countries, the same methods of

deceiving the credulity, and of affecting the services, of mankind; but it must ingeniously be confessed that the ministers of the Catholic Church imitated the profane model which they were impatient to destroy. The most respectable bishops had persuaded themselves that the ignorant rustics would more cheerfully renounce the superstitions of Paganism, if they found some resemblance, some compensation, in the bosom of Christianity. The religion of Constantine achieved, in less than a century, the final conquest of the Roman empire; but the victors themselves were insensibly subdued by the arts of their vanquished rivals." (Gibbon, "Decline and Fall of the Roman Empire," Ch. XXVIII.)

3. EARLY FORM OF CHRISTIAN BAPTISM. History furnishes ample proof that in the first century after the death of Christ, baptism was administered solely by immersion. Tertullian thus refers to the immersion ceremony common in his day: "There is no difference whether one is washed in a sea or in a pool, in a river or in a fountain, in a lake or in a channel; nor is there any difference between those whom John dipped in Jordan, and those whom Peter dipped in the Tiber. * * * We are immersed in the water."

Justin Martyr describes the ceremony as practiced by himself. First describing the preparatory examination of the candidate, he proceeds: "After that they are led by us to where there is water, and are born again in that kind of new birth by which we ourselves were born again. For in the name of God, the Father and the Lord of all, and of Jesus Christ, our Savior, and of the Holy Spirit, the immersion in water is performed; because the Christ hath also said, 'Except a man be born again, he cannot enter into the kingdom of heaven.'"

Bishop Bennet says concerning the practices of the early Christians: "They led them into the water and laid them down in the water as a man is laid in a grave; and then they said those words, 'I baptize (or wash) thee in the name of the Father, Son, and Holy Ghost;' then they raised them up again, and clean garments were put on them; from whence came the phrases of being baptized into Christ's death, of being buried with Him by baptism into death, of our being risen with Christ, and of our putting on the Lord Jesus Christ, of putting off the old man, and putting on the new."

"That the apostles immersed whom they baptized there is no doubt. * * * And that the ancient church followed their example is very clearly evinced by innumerable testimonies of the fathers." (Vossius.)

"Burying as it were the person baptized in the water, and raising him out again, without question was anciently the more usual method." (Archbishop Secker.)

" 'Immersion' was the usual method in which baptism was administered in the early Church. * * * Immersion was undoubtedly a common mode of administering baptism, and was not discontinued when infant baptism prevailed. * * * * * Sprinkling gradually took the place of immersion without any formal renunciation of the latter." (Canon Farrar.)

4. HISTORICAL NOTES ON INFANT BAPTISM. "The baptism of infants, in the first two centuries after Christ, was altogether unknown. * * * The custom of baptizing infants did not begin before the third age after Christ was born. In the former ages no trace of it appears; and it was introduced without the command of Christ." (Curcullaeus.)

"It is certain that Christ did not ordain infant baptism. * * * We cannot prove that the apostles ordained infant baptism. From those places where baptism of a whole family is mentioned (as in Acts xvi, 33; I Cor. i, 16) we can draw no such conclusion, because the inquiry is still to be made, whether there were any children in the families of such an age that they were not capable of any intelligent reception of Christianity; for this is the only point on which the case turns. * * * * As baptism was closely united with a conscious entrance on Christian communion, faith and baptism were always connected with one another; and thus it is in the highest degree probable that baptism was performed only in instances where both could meet together, and that the practice of infant baptism was unknown at this (the apostolic) period. * * * That not till so late a period as (at least certainly not earlier than) Irenaeus, a trace of infant baptism appears; and that it first became recognized as an apostolic tradition in the course of the third century, is evidence rather against than for the admission of its apostolic origin." (Johann Neander, a German theologian who flourished in the first half of the nineteenth century.)

"Let them therefore come when they are grown up—when they can understand—when they are taught whither they are to come. Let them become Christians when they can know Christ." (Tertullian, one of the Latin "Christian Fathers;" he lived from 150 to 220 A. D.) Tertullian's almost violent opposition to the practice of pedobaptism is cited by Neander as "a proof that it was then not usually considered an apostolic ordinance; for in that case he would hardly have ventured to speak so strongly against it."

Martin Luther, writing in the early part of the sixteenth century, declared: "It cannot be proven by the sacred scriptures that infant baptism was instituted by Christ, or begun by the first Christians after the apostles."

"By *tekna* the Apostle understands, not infants, but posterity; in which signification the word occurs in many places of the New Testament (see among others John viii, 39); whence it appears that the argument which is very commonly taken from this passage for the baptism of infants, is of no force, and good for nothing." (Limborch, a native of Holland, and a theologian of repute; he lived 1633–1712.)

5. SUMMARY OF CHANGES IN THE SACRAMENT AS AN ORDINANCE. "Errors concerning the sacrament, and its signification, and the manner of administering it, grew rapidly in the professed Christian churches during the early centuries of the Christian era. As soon as the power of the priesthood had departed, much disputation arose in matters of ordinance, and the observance of the sacrament became distorted. Theological teachers strove to foster the idea that there was much mystery attending this naturally simple and most impressive ordinance; that all who were not in full communion with the Church should be excluded, not only from participation in the ordinance, which was justifiable, but from the privilege of witnessing the service, lest they profane the mystic rite by their unhallowed

presence. Then arose the heresy of transubstantiation,—which held that the sacramental emblems by the ceremony of consecration lost their natural character of simple bread and wine, and became in reality flesh and blood,—actually parts of the crucified body of Christ. Arguments against such dogmas is useless. Then followed the veneration of the emblems by the people, the bread and wine—regarded as part of Christ's tabernacle, being elevated in the mass for the adoration of the people; and later, the custom of suppressing half of the sacrament was introduced. By the innovation last mentioned, only the bread was administered, the dogmatic assertion being that both the body and the blood were represented in some mystical way in one of the "elements." Certain it is, that Christ required his disciples to both eat and drink in remembrance of Him." (The Author, "Articles of Faith," Lecture 9, Note 4.)

6. AS TO THE ANTIQUITY OF THE DOCTRINE OF TRANSUBSTANTIATION. As stated in the text, the date of origin of the Catholic doctrine of transubstantiation has been much debated. The following summary is instructive. "Protestants combatting the Catholic idea of the real presence of the flesh and blood in the eucharist—transubstantiation— have endeavored to prove that this doctrine was not of earlier origin than the eighth century. In this, however, the evidence is against them. Ignatius, bishop of Antioch, writing early in the second century, says of certain supposed heretics: 'They do not admit of eucharists and oblations, because they do not believe the eucharist to be the flesh of our Savior Jesus Christ, who suffered for our sins.' (Epistles of Ignatius to the Smyrneans.) So Justin Martyr, also writing in the first half of the second century: 'We do not receive them [the bread and the wine] as ordinary food or ordinary drink, but as by the word of God, Jesus Christ, our Savior, was made flesh and took upon him both flesh and blood for our salvation, so also the food which was blessed by the prayer of the word which proceeded from him, and from which our flesh and blood, by transmutation, receive nourishment, is, we are taught, both the flesh and blood of that Jesus who was made flesh.' (Justin's Apology to Emperor Antoninus.) After Justin's time the testimony of the

fathers is abundant. There can be no doubt as to the antiquity of the idea of the real presence of the body and blood of Jesus in the eucharist; but that proves—as we said of infant baptism—not that the doctrine is true, but that soon after the apostles had passed away, the simplicity of the gospel was corrupted or else entirely departed from." (B. H. Roberts, "Outlines of Ecclestiastical History," p. 133.)

CHAPTER IX.

1. Among the controlling causes leading to the general apostasy of the Church we have specified as third in the series: *Unauthorized changes in Church organization and government.*

2. A comparison between the plan of organization on which the Primitive Church was founded and the ecclesiastical system which took its place will afford valuable evidence as to the true or apostate condition of the modern Church. The Primitive Church was officered by apostles, pastors, high priests, seventies, elders, bishops, priests, teachers, and deacons.[a] We have no evidence that the presiding council of the Church, comprising the twelve apostles, was continued beyond the earthly ministry of those who had been ordained to that holy calling during the life of Christ or soon after His ascension. Nor is there record of any ordination of individuals to the apostleship, irrespective of membership in the council of twelve, beyond those whose calling and ministry are chronicled in the New Testament, which, as a historical record, ends with the first century.

3. Ecclesiastical history other than the holy scriptures informs us, however, that wherever a branch, or church, was organized, a bishop or an elder (presbyter) was placed in charge. There is no doubt that while the apostles lived,

---

[a]See Luke 6: 13 and Mark 3: 14; Eph. 4: 11; Heb. 5: 1-5; Luke 10: 1-11; Acts 14: 23; 15: 6; I Peter 5: 1; I Tim. 3: 1; Titus 1: 7; Rev. 1: 6; Acts 13: 1; I Tim. 3: 8-12.

they were recognized and respected as the presiding authorities of the Church. As they established branches or churches, they selected the bishops, and submitted their nominations to the vote of the members. As already stated, the principle of self-government, or common consent, was respected in apostolic days with a care amounting to sacred duty. We read that the bishops were assisted in their local administration by presbyters and deacons.

4. After the apostles had gone, bishops and other officers were nominated by, or at the instance of, the existing authorities. The affairs of each church or branch were conducted and regulated by the local officers, so that a marked equality existed among the several churches, none exercising or claiming supremacy except as to the deference voluntarily paid to those churches that had been organized by the personal ministry of the apostles. Throughout the first and the greater part of the second century, "the Christian churches were independent on each other; nor were they joined together by association, confederacy, or other bonds but those of charity. Each Christian assembly was a little state, governed by its own laws, which were either enacted, or, at least, approved by the society."[b]

5. As with the churches, so with their bishops,—there was a recognized equality among them. Late in the second, and throughout the third century, however, marked distinctions and recognition of rank arose among the bishops, those of large and wealthy cities assuming authority and dignity above that accorded by them to the bishops of the country provinces. The bishops of the largest cities or provinces, took to themselves the distinguishing title of

---

[b]Mosheim, "Eccl. Hist.," Cent. II, Part II, ch. 2: 2.

Metropolitans,[c] and assumed a power of presidency over the bishops of more limited jurisdiction.

6.   The second century was marked by the custom of holding synods or church councils; the practice originated among the churches in Greece, and thence became general. These councils grew rapidly in power, so that in the third century we find them legislating for the churches, and directing by edict and command, in matters which formerly had been left to the vote of the people. Needless to say that with such assumptions of authority came arrogance and tyranny in the government of the Church. As the form of church government changed more and more, many minor orders of clergy or church officers arose; thus in the third century we read of sub-deacons, acolytes, ostiars, readers, exorcists, and copiates. As an instance of the pride of office, it is worthy of note that a sub-deacon was forbidden to sit in the presence of a deacon without the latter's express consent.

7.   Rome, so long the "mistress of the world" in secular affairs, arrogated to herself a pre-eminence in church matters, and the bishop of Rome claimed supremacy. It is doubtless true that the church at Rome was organized by Peter and Paul. Tradition, founded on error, said that the apostle Peter was the first bishop of Rome; and those who successively were acknowledged as bishops of the metropolis claimed to be, in fact, lineal successors of the presiding apostle. The high but none the less false claim is made by the Catholic Church in this day, that the present pope is the last lineal successor—not alone to the bishopric but to the apostleship.

---

[c]See Mosheim, "Eccl. Hist.," Cent. II, Part II, ch. 2: 3; also Cent. IV, Part II, ch. 2: 3, and compare Cent. I, Part II, ch. 2: 14.

8. The rightful supremacy of the bishops of Rome, or Roman pontiffs as they came to be known, was early questioned; and when Constantine made Byzantium, or Constantinople, the capital of the empire, the bishop of Constantinople claimed equality. The dispute divided the Church, and for five hundred years the dissension increased, until in the ninth century (855 A. D.) it developed into a great disruption, in consequence of which the bishop of Constantinople, known distinctively as the patriarch, disavowed all further allegiance to the bishop of Rome, otherwise known as the Roman pontiff. This disruption is marked today by the distinction between Roman Catholics and Greek Catholics.

9. The election of pontiff, or bishop of Rome, was long left to the vote of the people and clergy; later the electoral function was vested in the clergy alone; and in the eleventh century the power was lodged in the college of cardinals, where it remains vested today. The Roman pontiffs strove with unremitting zeal to acquire temporal as well as spiritual authority; and their influence had become so great that in the eleventh century we find them claiming the right to direct princes, kings, and emperors in the affairs of the several nations. It was at this, the early period of their greatest temporal power, that the pontiffs took the title of *Pope*, the word meaning literally papa, or father, and applied in the sense of universal parent. The power of the popes was increased during the twelfth century, and may be said to have reached its height in the thirteenth century.

10. Not content with assumed supremacy in all church affairs, the popes "carried their insolent pretensions so far as to give themselves out for lords of the universe, arbiters of the fate of kingdoms and empires, and supreme rulers

over the kings and princes of the earth."[d] They claimed
the right to authorize and direct in the internal affairs of
nations, and to make lawful the rebellion of subjects against
their rulers if the latter failed to keep favor with the papal
power.

11.   Compare this arrogant and tyrannical church of the
world with the Church of Christ. Unto Pilate our Lord declared, "My kingdom is not of this world;"[e] and on an
earlier occasion, when the people would have proclaimed
Him king with earthly dominion,[f] He departed from them.
Yet the Church that boasts of its divine origin as founded
by the Christ, who would not be a king, lifts itself above all
kings and rulers, and proclaims itself the supreme power in
the affairs of nations.

12.   In the fourth century the Church had promulgated
what has been since designated as an infamy, viz: that
"errors in religion, when maintained and adhered to after
proper admonition, were punishable with civil penalties,
and corporeal tortures."[g] The effect of this unjust rule appeared as more and more atrocious with the passage of the
years, so that in the eleventh century, and later, we find the
Church imposing punishment of fine, imprisonment, bodily
torture, and even death, as penalties for infraction of church
regulations, and, more infamous still, providing for mitiga-
tion or annulment of such sentences on payment of money.
This led to the shocking practice of selling *indulgences*
or pardons, which custom was afterward carried to the
awful extreme of issuing such before the commission of the

[d]Mosheim, "Eccl. Hist.," Cent. XI, Part II, ch. 2: 2.
[e]John 18: 36.
[f]John 6: 15.
[g]Mosheim, "Eccl. Hist.," Cent. IV, Part II, ch. 3: 16.

specific offense, thus literally offering for sale licenses to sin, with assurance of temporal and promise of spiritual immunity.

13. The granting of indulgences as exemptions from temporal penalties was at first confined to the bishops and their agents, and the practice dates as an organized traffic from about the middle of the twelfth century. It remained for the popes, however, to go to the blasphemous extreme of assuming to remit the penalties of the hereafter on payment of the sums prescribed. Their pretended justification of the impious assumption was as horrible as the act itself, and constitutes the dreadful *doctrine of supererogation*.

14. As formulated in the thirteenth century, this doctrine was thus set forth: "That there actually existed an immense treasure of *merit*, composed of the pious deeds and virtuous actions which the saints had performed *beyond what was necessary for their own salvation*, and which were therefore applicable to the benefit of others; that the guardian and dispenser of this precious treasure was the Roman pontiff, and that of consequence he was empowered to assign to such as he thought proper a portion of this inexhaustible source of merit, suitable to their respective guilt, and sufficient to deliver them from the punishment due to their crimes."[h]

15. The doctrine of supererogation is as unreasonable as it is unscriptural and untrue. Man's individual responsibility for his acts is as surely a fact as is his agency to act for himself. He will be saved through the merits and by the atoning sacrifice of our Redeemer and Lord; and his

[h]As cited by Mosheim; see "Eccl. Hist.," Cent. XII, Part II, ch. 3: 4.

claim upon the salvation provided is strictly dependent on his compliance with the principles and ordinances of the gospel as established by Jesus Christ. Remission of sins and the eventual salvation of the human soul are provided for; but these gifts of God are not to be purchased with money. Compare the awful fallacies of supererogation and the blasphemous practice of assuming to remit the sins of one man in consideration of the merits of another, with the declaration of the one and only Savior of mankind: "But I say unto you that every idle word that men shall speak, they shall give an account thereof in the day of judgment."[i] His inspired apostle, seeing in prophetic vision the day of awful certainty, solemnly testifies, "And I saw the dead, small and great stand before God; and the books were opened, and another book was opened, which is the book of life, and the dead were judged out of those things which were written in the books, *according to their works*. And the sea gave up the dead which were in it; and death and hell delivered up the dead which were in them; *and they were judged every man according to their works*."[j]

16. The scriptures proclaim the eternal fact of individual accountability;[k] the Church in the days of its degeneracy declares that the merit of one may be bought by another and paid for in worldly coin. Can such a Church be in any measure the Church of Christ?

17. In illustration of the indulgences as sold in Germany in the sixteenth century, we have the record of the doings of John Tetzel, agent of the pope, who traveled

---

[i]Matt. 12: 36.

[j]Rev. 20: 12, 13. Italics introduced.

[k]For a concise treatment of the doctrine of man's responsibility see the author's "Articles of Faith," Lecture 3.

about selling forgiveness of sins. Says Milner: "Myconius assures us that he himself heard Tetzel declaim with incredible effrontery concerning the unlimited power of the pope and the efficacy of indulgences. The people believed that the moment any person had paid the money for the indulgence he became certain of his salvation; and that the souls for whom the indulgences were bought, were instantly released out of purgatory. * * * John Tetzel boasted that he had saved more souls from hell by his indulgences than St. Peter had converted to Christianity by his preaching. He assured the purchasers of them, their crimes, however enormous, would be forgiven; whence it became almost needless for him to bid them dismiss all fears concerning their salvation. For, remission of sins being fully obtained, what doubt could there be of salvation?"[1]

18. A copy of an indulgence written by the hand of Tetzel, the vendor of popish pardons, has been preserved to us as follows: "May our Lord, Jesus Christ, have mercy upon thee and absolve thee by the merits of his most holy passion. And I, by his authority, that of his Apostles Peter and Paul, and of the most holy pope granted and committed to me in these parts, do absolve thee, first from all ecclesiastical censures, in whatever manner they have been incurred; and then from all the sins, transgressions, and excesses, how enormous soever they may be, even for such as are reserved for the cognizance of the holy see; and as far as the keys of the holy church extend, I remit to thee all the punishment which thou deservest in purgatory on their account; and I restore thee to the holy sacraments of the church, to the unity of the faithful, and to that innocence and purity which thou possessedst at baptism; so that when

---

[1]Milner, "History of the Church," Cent. XVI, ch. 2.

thou diest, the gates of punishment shall be shut, and the gates of the paradise of delight shall be opened; and if thou shalt not die at present, this grace shall remain in full force when thou art at the point of death. In the name of the Father and of the Son and of the Holy Ghost."[m]

19. By way of excuse or defense, it has been claimed for the Roman Catholic Church that a profession of contrition or repentance was required of every applicant for indulgence, and that the pardon was issued on the basis of such penitence, and not primarily for money or its equivalent; but that recipients of indulgences, at first voluntarily, and later in compliance with established custom, made a material offering or donation to the Church. It is reported, moreover, that some of the abuses with which the selling of indulgences had been associated were disapproved by the Council of Trent, about the middle of the sixteenth century. Nevertheless, the dread fact remains that for four hundred years the Church had claimed for its pope the power to remit all sins, and that the promise of remission had been sold and bought.[n]

20. The awful sin of blasphemy consists in taking to one's self the divine prerogatives and powers. Here we find the pope of Rome, the head of the only church recognized at the time, assuming to remit the punishments due in the hereafter for sins committed in mortality. A pope assuming to sit in judgment as God himself! Is this not a fulfilment of the dread conditions of apostasy foreseen and foretold as antecedent to the second advent of Christ? Read for yourselves: "Let no man deceive you by any means: for that day shall not come, except there come a falling

---

[m]Milner, "Church History," Cent. XVI, ch. 2.
[n]See Note 1, end of chapter.

away first, and that man of sin be revealed, the son of per-dition; *who opposeth and exalteth himself above all that is called God, or that is worshiped; so that he as God sitteth in the temple of God, shewing himself that he is God.*"[o]

21.   Another abuse perpetrated by the councils through which assemblies the supreme pontiffs exercised their auto-cratic powers, is seen in the restrictions placed on the read-ing and interpretation of scripture. The same Council of Trent, which had disclaimed authority or blame for the acts of church officials regarding the scandalous traffic in indul-gences, prescribed most rigid regulations forbidding the reading of the scriptures by the people. Thus: "A severe and intolerable law was enacted, with respect to all inter-preters and expositors of the scriptures, by which they were forbidden to explain the sense of these divine books, in matters of faith and practice, in such a manner as to make them speak a different language from that of the church and the ancient doctors. The same law farther declared that the church alone (i. e. its ruler, the Roman pontiff) had the right of determining the true meaning and signification of scripture. To fill up the measure of these tyrannical and iniquitous proceedings, the church of Rome persisted ob-stinately in affirming, though not always with the same im-prudence and plainness of speech, that *the holy scriptures were not composed for the use of the multitude, but only for that of their spiritual teachers;* and, of consequence, ordered these divine records to be taken from the people in all places where it was allowed to execute its imperious demands."[p]

---

[o]Thess. 2: 3, 4. Italics introduced. See Note 4, end of chapter.

[p]Mosheim, "Eccl. Hist., Cent. XVI, Part I, ch. 1: 25. The Italics are introduced by the present writer.

22. Is it possible that a church teaching such heresies can be the Church established by Jesus Christ? The Lord Jesus commanded all: *"Search the scriptures, for in them ye think ye have eternal life; and they are they which testify of me."*[q]

23. Surely a pall of darkness had fallen upon the earth. The Church of Christ had long since ceased to exist. In place of a priesthood conferred by divine authority, a man-created papacy ruled with the iron hand of tyranny and without regard to moral restraint. In a scholarly work Dr. J. W. Draper gives a list of pontiffs who had stood at the head of the Church from the middle of the eighth to the middle of the eleventh centuries, with biographical notes of each.[r] And what a picture is there outlined! To win the papal crown no crime was too great, and for a period of centuries the immoralities of many of the popes and their subordinates are too shocking for detailed description. It may be claimed that the author last cited, and whose words are given below, was an avowed opponent of the Roman Catholic Church, and that, therefore, his judgment is prejudiced; in reply let it be said that the attested facts of history support the dread arraignment. In commenting on the facts set forth, Dr. Draper says:

24. "More than a thousand years had elapsed since the birth of our Savior, and such was the condition of Rome. Well may the historian shut the annals of those times in disgust. Well may the heart of the Christian sink within him at such a catalogue of hideous crimes. Well may we ask,

[q]John 5: 39; compare verse 46; also Isaiah 8: 20; Luke 16: 29; and Acts 17: 11.

[r]See Note 3, end of chapter.

Were these the vicegerents of God upon earth—these, who had truly reached the goal beyond which the last effort of human wickedness cannot pass? Not until several centuries after these events did public opinion come to the true and philosophical conclusion—the total rejection of the divine claims of the papacy. For a time the evils were attributed to the manner of the pontifical election, as if that could by any possibility influence the descent of a power which claimed to be supernatural and under the immediate care of God. * * No one can study the development of the Italian ecclesiastical power without discovering how completely it depended on human agency, too often on human passion and intrigue; how completely wanting it was of any mark of the Divine construction and care—the offspring of man, not of God, and therefore bearing upon it the lineaments of human passions, human virtues, and human sins."[*]

25. By increasing changes and unauthorized alterations in organization and government, the earthly establishment known as "the Church," with popes, cardinals, abbots, friars, monks, exorcists, acolytes, etc., lost all semblance to the Church as established by Christ and maintained by His apostles. The Catholic argument that there has been an uninterrupted succession of authority in the priesthood from the Apostle Peter to the present occupant of the papal throne, is untenable in the light of history, and unreasonable in the light of fact. Authority to speak and act in the name of God, power to officiate in the saving ordinances of the gospel of Christ, the high privilege of serving as a duly commissioned ambassador of the court of Heaven,—these are not to be had as the gifts of princes, nor are they to be bought for money, nor can they be won as trophies of the

---

[*]Draper, "Intellectual Development of Europe; Vol. I., p. 382.

bloody sword. The history of the papacy is the condemnation of the Church of Rome.[t]

Notes.

1. THE ROMAN CHURCH RESPONSIBLE FOR THE TRAFFIC IN "INDULGENCES." In view of the claim asserted by some defenders of the Roman Church, to the effect that the shameful traffic in indulgences was not sanctioned by the church, and that the church cannot be held accountable for the excesses to which its subordinates may go in their alleged official acts, the following remarks by Milner, the judicious authority on Church History (Cent. XVI, chap. 2), may be of interest: "It does not appear that the rulers of the hierarchy ever found the least fault with Tetzel as exceeding his commission, till an opposition was openly made to the practice of indulgences. Whence it is evident, that the protestants have not unjustly censured the corruptions of the court of Rome in this respect. * * * The indulgences were farmed to the highest bidders, and the undertakers employed such deputies to carry on the traffic as they thought most likely to promote their lucrative views. The inferior officers concerned in this commerce were daily seen in public houses enjoying themselves in riot and voluptuousness (Maimbourg, p. 11). In fine, whatever the greatest enemy of popery could have wished, was at that time exhibited with the most undisguised impudence and temerity, as if on purpose to render that wicked ecclesiastical system infamous before all mankind."

The author proceeds to comment on the graded prices by which these indulgences were placed within the pecuniary reach of all classes, and finds in the wholesale traffic proof of profound ignorance and dire superstition, and then points out the need of a new gospel dispensation as follows: This, however, was the very situation of things *which opened the way for the reception of the gospel.* But who was to proclaim the gospel in its native beauty and simplicity? The princes, the bishops, and the learned men of the times saw all this scandalous traffic respecting the pardon of sins; but none was found who possessed the knowledge, the courage, and the honesty,

---

[t]See Notes 2 and 3, end of chapter.

necessary to detect the fraud, and to lay open to mankind the true doctrine of salvation by the remission of sins through Jesus Christ." Milner finds the inauguration of a new era in the "Reformation" during the sixteenth century. It is sufficient for our present purpose to know that he recognized the need of preparation whereby the way would be opened "for the reception of the gospel." (Milner, "Ch. Hist.," Cent. XVI, ch. 2; italics introduced.)

2. THREE POPES AT ONE TIME. "One of the severest blows given both the temporal and the spiritual authority of the popes, was the removal, in 1309, through the influence of the French king, Philip the Fair, of the papal chair from Rome to Avignon, in Provence, near the frontier of France. Here it remained for a space of about seventy years, an era known in church history as the Babylonian Captivity. While it was established here, all the popes were French, and of course all their policies were shaped and controlled by the French kings. * * * * The discontent awakened among the Italians by the situation of the papal court at length led to an open rupture between them and the French party. In 1378 the opposing factions each elected a pope, and thus there were two heads of the church, one at Avignon and the other at Rome. The spectacle of *two rival popes,* each claiming to be the rightful successor of St. Peter, and the sole infallible head of the Church, very naturally led men to question the claims and infallibility of both. It gave the reverence which the world had so generally held for the Roman See a rule shock, and one from which it never recovered. Finally, in 1409, a general council of the church assembled at Pisa, for the purpose of composing the shameful quarrel. The council deposed both popes, and elected Alexander V as the supreme head of the church. But matters, instead of being mended hereby were only made worse; for neither of the deposed pontiffs would lay down his authority in obedience to the demands of the council, and consequently *there were now three popes instead of two.* In 1414 another council was called, at Constance, for the settlement of the growing dispute. Two of the claimants were deposed and one resigned. A new pope was then elected— Pope Martin V. In his person the Catholic world was again united under a single spiritual head. The schism was outwardly healed, but the wound had been too deep not to leave permanent marks upon the church." (P. V. N. Myers, "Gen. Hist.," pp. 457, 458 Italics introduced.)

The rupture between the French and Italian factions, referred to by Myers in the quotation given above, is known in history as the Great Schism. It may be regarded as the decisive beginning of decline in the temporal power of the popes.

3. THE PAPACY CONDEMNS ITSELF. The line of succession in the papacy for a limited period as referred to in the text, is given by Draper as follows:

"To some it might seem, considering the interests of religion alone, desirable to omit all biographical reference to the popes; but this cannot be done with justice to the subject. The essential principle of the papacy, that the Roman pontiff is the vicar of Christ upon earth, necessarily obtrudes his personal relation upon us. How shall we understand his faith unless we see it illustrated in his life? Indeed, the unhappy character of those relations was the inciting cause of the movements in Germany, France, and England, ending in the extinction of the papacy as an actual political power, movements to be understood only through a sufficient knowledge of the private lives and opinions of the popes. It is well, as far as possible, to abstain from burdening systems with the imperfections of individuals. In this case they are inseparably interwoven. The signal peculiarity of the papacy is that, though its history may be imposing, its biography is infamous. I shall, however, forbear to speak of it in this latter respect more than the occasion seems necessarily to require; shall pass in silence some of those cases which would profoundly shock my religious reader, and therefore restrict myself to the ages between the middle of the eighth and the middle of the eleventh centuries, excusing myself to the impartial critic by the apology that these were the ages with which I have been chiefly concerned in this chapter.

"On the death of Pope Paul I, who had attained the pontificate A. D. 757, the Duke of Nepi compelled some bishops to consecrate Constantine, one of his brothers, as pope; but more legitimate electors subsequently, A. D. 768, choosing Stephen IV, the usurper and his adherents were severely punished; the eyes of Constantine were put out; the tongue of the Bishop Theodorus was amputated, and he was left in a dungeon to expire in the agonies of thirst. The nephews of Pope Adrian seized his successor, Pope Leo III, A. D.

795, in the street, and, forcing him into a neighboring church, attempted to put out his eyes and cut out his tongue; at a later period, this pontiff, trying to suppress a conspiracy to depose him, Rome became the scene of rebellion, murder and conflagration. His successor, Stephen V, A. D. 816, was ignominiously driven from the city; his successor, Paschal I, was accused of blinding and murdering two ecclesiastics in the Lateran Palace; it was necessary that imperial commissioners should investigate the matter, but the pope died, after having exculpated himself by oath before thirty bishops. John VIII, A. D. 872, unable to resist the Mohammedans, was compelled to pay them tribute; the Bishop of Naples, maintaining a secret alliance with them, received his share of the plunder they collected. Him John excommunicated, nor would he give him absolution unless he would betray the chief Mohammedans and assassinate others himself. There was an ecclesiastical conspiracy to murder the pope; some of the treasures of the church were seized; and the gate of St. Pancrazia was opened with false keys, to admit the Saracens into the city. Formosus, who had been engaged in these transactions, and excommunicated as a conspirator for the murder of John, was subsequently elected pope, A. D. 891; he was succeeded by Boniface VI, A. D. 896, who had been deposed from the diaconate, and again from the priesthood, for his immoral and lewd life. By Stephen VII, who followed, the dead body of Formosus was taken from the grave, clothed in the papal habilaments, propped up in a chair, tried before a council, and the preposterous and indecent scene completed by cutting off three of the fingers of the corpse and casting it into the Tiber; but Stephen himself was destined to exemplify how low the papacy had fallen: he was thrown into prison and strangled. In the course of five years, from A. D. 896 to A. D. 900, five popes were consecrated. Leo V, who succeeded in A. D. 904, was in less than two months thrown into prison by Christopher, one of his chaplains, who usurped his place, and who, in his turn, was shortly expelled from Rome by Sergius III, who, by the aid of a military force, seized the pontificate, A. D. 905. This man, according to the testimony of the times, lived in criminal intercourse with the prostitute Theodora, who, with her daughters Marozia and Theodora, also prostitutes, exercised an extraordinary control over him. The love of Theodora was also shared by John X: she gave him first the archbishopric of Ravenna, and then translated him to Rome, A. D. 915, as pope. John was not unsuited to the times; he organized a confederacy which perhaps prevented Rome from being captured by the Saracens, and the world was astonished and edified by the appearance of this warlike pontiff at the head of his troops. By the love of Theodora, as was said, he had maintained himself in the papacy for fourteen years; by the intrigues and hatred of her daughter Marozia he was overthrown. She surprised him in the Lateran Palace; killed his brother Peter before his face; threw him into prison, where he soon died, smothered, as was asserted, with a pillow. After a short interval Marozia made her own son pope as John XI, A. D. 931. Many affirmed that Pope Sergius was his father, but she herself inclined to attribute him to her husband Alberic, whose brother Guido she subsequently married. Another of her sons, Alberic, so called from his supposed father, jealous of his brother John, cast him and their mother Marozia into prison. After a time Alberic's son was elected pope A. D. 956; he assumed the title of John XII, the amorous Marozia thus having given a son and a grandson to the papacy. John was only nineteen years old when he thus became the head of Christendom. His reign was characterized by the most shocking immoralities, so that the Emperor Otho I was compelled by the German clergy to interfere. A synod was summoned for his trial in the Church of St. Peter, before which it appeared that John had received bribes for the consecration of bishops; that he had ordained one who was but ten years old, and had performed that ceremony over another in a stable; he was charged with incest with one of his father's concubines, and with so many adulteries that the Lateran Palace had become a brothel; he put out the eyes of one ecclesiastic, and castrated another, both dying in consequence of their injuries; he was given to drunkenness, gambling and the invocation of Jupiter and Venus. When cited to appear before the council, he sent word that 'he had gone out hunting;' and to the fathers who remonstrated with him, he threateningly remarked 'that Judas, as well as the other disciples, received from his Master the power of binding and loosing, but that as soon as he proved a traitor to the common cause, the only power he retained was that of binding his own neck.' Hereupon he was deposed, and Leo VIII elected in his stead, A. D. 963; but subsequently getting the upper hand, he seized his antagonists, cut off the hand of one, the nose, finger, tongue of others. His life was eventually brought to an end by the vengeance of a man whose wife he had seduced.

"After such details it is almost needless to allude to the annals of succeeding popes: to relate that John XIII was strangled in prison; that Boniface VII imprisoned Benedict VII and killed him by starvation; that John XIV was secretly put to death in the dungeons of the Castle of St. Angelo; that the corpse of Boniface was dragged by the populace through the streets. The sentiment of reverence for the sovereign pontiff, nay, even of respect, had become extinct in Rome; throughout Europe the clergy were so shocked at the state of things, that, in their indignation, they began to look with approbation on the intention of the Emperor Otho to take from the Italians their privilege of appointing the successor of St. Peter, and confine it to his own family. But his kinsman, Gregory V, whom he placed on the pontifical throne, was very soon compelled by the Romans to fly; his excommunications and religious thunders were turned into derision by them; they were too well acquainted with the true nature of those terrors; they were living behind the scenes. A terrible punishment awaited the Anti-pope John XVI. Otho returned into Italy, seized him, put out his eyes, cut off his nose and tongue, and sent him through the streets mounted on an ass, with his face to the tail, and a wine-bladder on his head. It seemed impossible that things could become worse: yet Rome had still to see Benedict IX, A. D. 1033, a boy of less than twelve years, raised to the apostolic throne. Of this pontiff, one of his successors, Victor III, declared that his life was so shameful, so foul, so execrable, that he shuddered to describe it. He ruled like a captain of banditti rather than a prelate. The people at last, unable to bear his adulteries, homicides, and abominations any longer, rose against him. In despair of maintaining his position, he put up the papacy at auction. It was bought by a presbyter named John, who became Gregory VI, A. D. 1045." (J. W. Draper, "Intellectual Development of Europe," Vol. I, ch. XII, pp. 378-381.)

4. COMMENTARY ON THE PASSAGE FROM II THESS. 2: 3, 4. It should be remembered that the application of Paul's declaration as to the apostasy made in the text, is the one generally made by theologians of Protestant denominations. It is in no way peculiar to the Church of Jesus Christ of Latter-day Saints. Let us read the passage

again: "Let no man deceive you by any means: for that day [the day of Christ's promised advent] shall not come except there come a falling away first, and that man of sin be revealed, the son of perdition, who opposeth and exalteth himself above all that is called God, or that is worshiped, so that he as God sitteth in the temple of God, shewing himself that he is God."

In his Bible Commentary, Dr. Adam Clarke says of this scripture: "The general run of Protestant writers understand the whole as referring to the popes and church of Rome, or the whole system of the papacy. * * * Bishop Newton has examined the whole prophecy with his usual skill and judgment. * * * The principle part of modern commentators follow his steps. He applies the whole to the Romish church: the apostasy, its defection from the pure doctrines of Christianity; and the 'man of sin,' etc., the general succession of the popes of Rome." An abridgment of Bishop Newton's interpretation is then added; this, in part, is as follows:

"*For that day shall not come except, etc.*—The day of Christ shall not come except there come the apostasy first. The apostasy here described is plainly not of a civil, but of a religious nature; not a revolt from the government, but a defection from the true religion and worship. * * *

"*So that he as God sitteth in the temple, etc.*—By the temple of God the apostle could not well mean the temple of Jerusalem, because that, he knew, would be destroyed within a few years. After the death of Christ, the temple of Jerusalem is never called the temple of God; and if, at any time, they make mention of the house or temple of God, they mean the church in general or every particular believer. Whoever will consult I Cor. 3: 16, 17; II Cor. 6: 16; I Tim. 3: 15; Rev. 3: 12, will want no examples to prove that under the gospel dispensation, the temple of God is the Church of Christ; and the man of sin's sitting implies his ruling and presiding there. * * *

"Upon this survey, there appears little room to doubt of the general sense and meaning of the passage. The Thessalonians, (as we have seen from some expressions in the former epistle,) were alarmed as if the end of the world was at hand. The apostle, to correct their mistakes and dissipate their fears, assures them that a great apostasy or defection of the Christians from the true faith and worship must happen before the coming of Christ. This apostasy, all the concurrent marks and characters will justify us in charging upon the church of Rome. The true Christian worship is the worship of the only true God, through the one only Mediator, the man Christ Jesus, and from this worship the church of Rome has most notoriously departed, by substituting other mediators, and invoking and adoring saints and angels; nothing is apostasy if idolatry be not. ° ° ° If the apostasy be rightly charged upon the church of Rome, it follows, of consequence, that the 'man of sin' is the pope, not meaning any pope in particular, but the pope in general, as the chief head and supporter of this apostasy."

The opinion of Dr. MacKnight is also cited with approval by Clarke. In his "Commentary and Notes," (vol. III, p. 100, etc.) MacKnight says: "As it is said, the man of sin was *to be revealed in his season*, there can be little doubt that the dark ages, in which all learning was overturned by the irruption of the northern barbarians, were the season allotted to the man of sin for revealing himself. Accordingly we know, that in these ages, the corruptions of Christianity, and the usurpations of the clergy, were carried to the greatest height. In short, the annals of the world cannot produce persons and events to which the things written in this passage can be applied with so much fitness as to the bishops of Rome."

CHAPTER X.

RESULTS OF THE APOSTASY.—ITS SEQUEL.

1. The thoroughly apostate and utterly corrupt condition of the Church of Rome as proclaimed by its history down to the end of the fifteenth century,[a] was necessarily accompanied by absence of all spiritual sanctity and power whatever may have been the arrogant assumptions of the Church as to authority in spiritual affairs. Revolts against the Church, both as rebellion against her tyranny and in protest against her heresies, were not lacking. The most significant of these anti-church agitations arose in the connection with the awakening of intellectual activity which began in the latter part of the fourteenth century. The period from the tenth century onward to the time of the awakening has come to be known as the dark ages—characterized by stagnation in the progress of the useful arts and sciences as well as of fine arts and letters, and by a general condition of illiteracy and ignorance among the masses.

2. Ignorance is a fertile soil for evil growths, and the despotic government and doctrinal fallacies of the Church during this period of darkness were nourished by the ignorance of the times. With the change known in history as "the revival of learning" came the struggle for freedom from churchly tyranny.

3. One of the early revolts against the temporal and spiritual despotism of the papal Church was that of the

---

[a]See Note 1, end of chapter.

Albigenses in France during the thirteenth century. This uprising had been crushed by the papal autocracy with much cruelty and bloodshed. The next notable revolt was that of John Wickliffe in the fourteenth century. Wickliffe was a professor in Oxford university, England. He boldly assailed the ever-growing and greatly abused power of the monks, and denounced the corruption of the Church and the prevalence of doctrinal errors. He was particularly emphatic in his opposition to the papal restrictions as to the popular study of the scriptures, and gave to the world an English version of the Holy Bible translated from the Vulgate. In spite of persecution and sentence, he died a natural death; but years afterward the Church insisted on revenge, and in consequence, his bones were exhumed and burned, and the ashes scattered to the winds.

4. On the continent of Europe the agitation against the Church was carried on by John Huss and by Jerome of Prague, both of whom reaped martyrdom as the harvest of their righteous zeal. These instances are cited to show that though the Church had long been apostate to the core, there were men ready to sacrifice their lives in what they deemed to be the cause of truth.

5. Conditions existing at the opening of the sixteenth century have been concisely summarized by a modern historian as follows: "Previous to the opening of the sixteenth century there had been comparatively few—though there had been some, like the Albigenses in the south of France, the Wickliffites, in England, and the Hussites, in Bohemia —who denied the supreme and infallible authority of the bishop of Rome in all matters touching religion. Speaking in a very general manner it would be correct to say that at the close of the fifteenth century all the nations of West-

ern Europe professed the faith of the Latin or Roman Catholic Church, and yielded obedience to the Papal See."[b]

6.   The next notable revolt against the papal Church occurred in the sixteenth century, and assumed such proportions as to be designated the Reformation. The movement began in Germany about 1517, when Martin Luther, a monk of the Augustinian order and an instructor in the University of Wittenberg, publicly opposed and strongly denounced Tetzel, the shameless agent of papal indulgences. Luther was conscientious in his conviction that the whole system of church penances and indulgences was contrary to scripture, reason, and right. In line with the academic custom of the day—to challenge discussion and debate on disputed questions — Luther wrote his famous ninety-five theses against the practice of granting indulgences, and a copy of these he nailed to the door of Wittenberg church, inviting criticism thereon from all scholars. The news spread, and the theses were discussed in all scholastic centers of Europe. Luther then attacked other practices and doctrines of the Roman church, and the pope, Leo X, issued a "Bull" or papal decree against him, demanding an unconditional recantation on pain of excommunication from the Church. Luther publicly burned the pope's document, and thus declared his open revolt. The sentence of excommunication was pronounced.

7.   We cannot follow here in detail the doings of this bold reformer. Suffice it to say, he was not long left to fight

---

'Myers, "Gen. Hist.," p. 520.

single-handed. Among his able supporters was Phillip
Melanchthon, a professor in Wittenberg. Luther was summoned before a council or "Diet" at Worms in 1521. There
he openly declared for individual freedom of conscience.
There is inspiration in his words: "I cannot submit my
faith either to the pope or to the council, because it is as
clear as the day that they have frequently erred and contra-
dicted each other. Unless, therefore, I am convinced by
the testimony of scripture, or by the clearest reasoning—
unless I am persuaded by means of the passages I have
quoted,—and unless they thus render my conscience bound
by the word of God, I cannot and will not retract, for it
is unsafe for a Christian to speak against his conscience.
Here I stand, I can do no other, may God help me! Amen!"

8.   The religious controversy spread throughout Europe.
At the Second Diet of Spires (1529) an edict was issued
against the reformers; to this the representatives of seven
German principalities and other delegates entered a formal
protest, in consequence of which action the reformers were
henceforth known as *Protestants.* John, Elector of Saxony,
supported Luther in his opposition to papal authority, and
undertook the establishment of an independent church, the
constitution and plan of which were prepared at his instance by Luther and Melanchthon. Luther died in 1546,
but the work of revolution, if not in truth reformation, continued to grow. The Protestants, however, soon became divided among themselves, and broke up into many contending sects.

9.   In Switzerland, Ulrich Zwingli led in the movement
toward reform. He was accused of heresy, and when placed
on trial, he defended himself on the authority of the Bible as
against papal edict, and was for the time successful. The
contest was bitter, and in 1531 the Catholics and Protestants

of the region engaged in actual battle, in the which Zwingli was slain, and his body brutally mutilated.

10. John Calvin next appeared as the leader of the Swiss reformers, though he was an opponent of many of Zwingli's doctrines. He exerted great influence as a teacher, and is known as an extremist in doctrine. He advocated and vehemently defended the tenet of absolute predestination, thus denying the free agency of man. In France, Sweden, Denmark, and Holland, leaders arose and the Protestants became strong in their opposition to the Roman Church, though the several divisions were antagonistic to one another on many points of doctrine.

11. One effect of this Protestant uprising was the partial awakening of the Roman Church to the need of internal reform, and an authoritative restatement of Catholic principles was attempted. The movement was largely accomplished through the famous Council of Trent (1545-1563), which body disavowed for the Church the extreme claims made for "indulgences" and denied responsibility for many of the abuses with which the Church had been charged. But in connection with the attempted reform came a demand for more implicit obedience to the requirements of the Church.

12. Near the end of the fifteenth century, in the reign of Ferdinand and Isabella, the court of the Inquisition, then known as the Holy Office, had been established in Spain. The prime purpose of this secret tribunal was the detection and punishment of heresy. Of this infamous institution as operative in Spain, Myers says: "The Holy Office, as the tribunal was styled, thus became the instrument of the most incredible cruelty. Thousands were burned at the stake, and tens of thousands more condemned to endure penalties scarcely less terrible. Queen Isabella, in giving

her consent to the establishment of the tribunal in her dominions, was doubtless actuated by the purest religious zeal, and sincerely believed that in suppressing heresy she was discharging a simple duty, and rendering God good service. 'In the love of Christ and His Maid-Mother,' she says, 'I have caused great misery. I have depopulated towns and districts, provinces and kingdoms.' "[c]

13. Now, in the sixteenth century, in connection with the attempted reform in the doctrines of Catholicism, the terrible Inquisition, "assumed new vigor and activity, and heresy was sternly dealth with." Consider the following as throwing light on the conditions of that time: "At this point, in connection with the persecutions of the Inquisition, we should not fail to recall that in the sixteenth century a refusal to conform to the established worship was regarded by all, by Protestants as well as Catholics, as a species of treason against society and was dealt with accordingly. Thus we find Calvin at Geneva consenting to the burning of Servetus (1553) because he published views that the Calvinists thought heretical; and in England we see the Anglican Protestants waging the most cruel, bitter, and persistent persecutions, not only against the Catholics but also against all Protestants that refused to conform to the Established Church."[d]

14. What shall be said of a Church that seeks to propagate its faith by such methods? Are fire and sword the weapons with which truth fights her battles? Are torture and death the arguments of the gospel? However terrible the persecutions to which the early Church was subjected at the hands of heathen enemies, the persecutions waged by

[c]Myers, "Gen. Hist.," p. 500.
[d]Myers, "Gen. Hist.," p. 527.

the apostate church are far more terrible. Can such a church by any possibility be the Church of Christ? Heaven forbid!

15. In the revolts we have noted against the Church of Rome, notably in the Reformation, the zeal of the reformers led to many fallacies in the doctrines they advocated. Luther, himself, proclaimed the doctrine of absolute pre-destination and of justification by faith alone, thus nullify-ing belief in the God-given rights of free agency, and im-pairing the importance of individual effort.[e] Calvin and others were no less extreme. Nevertheless their ministry contributed to the awakening of individual conscience, and assisted in bringing about a measure of religious freedom of which the world had long been deprived.[f]

RISE OF THE CHURCH OF ENGLAND.

16. At the time of Martin Luther's revolt against the Church of Rome, Henry VIII reigned in England. In com-mon with all other countries of western Europe, Britain was profoundly stirred by the reformation movement. The king openly defended the Catholic Church and published a book in opposition to Luther's claims. This so pleased the pope, Leo X, that he conferred upon King Henry the distinguish-ing title, "Defender of the Faith." This took place about 1522, and from that time to the present, British sovereigns have proudly borne the title.

17. Within a few years after his accession to this title of distinction, we find King Henry among the bitterest enemies of the Roman Church, and the change came about in this wise. Henry desired a divorce from his wife, Queen Cath-

---

[e]See the Author's "Articles of Faith," Lecture 5.
[f]See Note 2, end of chapter.

erine, to give him freedom to marry Anne Boleyn. The pope hesitated in the matter of granting the divorce, and Henry, becoming impatient, disregarded the pope's authority and secretly married Anne Boleyn. The pope thereupon excommunicated the king from the Church. The English parliament, following the king's directions, passed the celebrated Act of Supremacy in 1534. This statute declared an absolute termination of all allegiance to papal authority, and proclaimed the king as supreme head of the Church in Britain. Thus originated the Church of England, without regard for or claim of divine authority, and without even a semblance of priestly succession.

18.   At first there was little innovation in doctrine or ritual in the newly formed church. It originated in revolt. Later a form of creed and a plan of organization were adopted, giving the Church of England some distinctive features. During the reigns of Edward VI, Queen Mary, and Queen Elizabeth, persecutions between Catholics and Protestants were extensive and violent. Several non-conformist sects arose, among them the Puritans and the Separatists. These were so persecuted that many of them fled to Holland as exiles. From among these came the notable colony of the Pilgrim Fathers, who crossed in the Mayflower to the shores of the then recently-discovered continent, and established themselves in America.

19.   The thoughtful student cannot fail to see in the progress of the great apostasy and its results the existence of an overruling power, operating toward eventual good, however mysterious its methods. The heart-rending persecutions to which the saints were subjected in the early centuries of our era, the anguish, the torture, the bloodshed, incurred in defense of the testimony of Christ, the rise of an apostate

church, blighting the intellect and leading captive the souls of men—all these dread scenes were foreknown to the Lord. While we cannot say or believe that such exhibitions of human depravity and blasphemy of heart were in accordance with the divine will, certainly God willed to permit full scope to the free agency of man, in the exercise of which agency some won the martyr's crown, and others filled the measure of their iniquity to overflowing.

20. Not less marked is the divine permission in the revolts and rebellions, in the revolutions and reformations, that developed in opposition to the darkening influence of the apostate church. Wycliffe and Huss, Luther and Melanchthon, Zwingli and Calvin, Henry VIII in his arrogant assumption of priestly authority, John Knox in Scotland, Roger Williams in America — these and a host of others builded better than they knew, in that their efforts laid in part the foundation of the structure of religious freedom and liberty of conscience,—and this in preparation for the restoration of the gospel as had been divinely predicted.

21. From the sixteenth century down to the present time, sects professedly founded on the tenets of Christianity have multiplied apace. They are now to be numbered by hundreds. On every side the claim has been heard, "Lo, here is Christ," or "Lo, there." There are churches named after their place of origin—as the Church of England; other sects are designated in honor of their famous promoters—as Lutherans, Calvinists, Wesleyans; others are known from some peculiarity of creed or doctrine—as Methodists, Presbyterians, and Baptists; but down to the beginning of the nineteenth century there was no church even claiming name or title as the Church of Christ. The only church existing at that time venturing to assert authority by suc-

cession was the Catholic Church, which as shown was wholly without priesthood or divine commission.

22. If the "Mother Church" be without divine authority or spiritual power, how can her children derive from her the right to officiate in the things of God? Who dares affirm the absurdity that man can originate for himself a priesthood which God shall honor and respect? Granted that men may, can and do, create among themselves societies, associations, sects, and churches if they choose so to designate their religious organizations; granted that they may formulate laws, prescribe rules, and construct elaborate plans of organization and government, and that all such laws, and rules and schemes of administration are binding upon those who voluntarily assume membership,—granted all these powers and rights— whence can such human creations derive the authority of the holy Priesthood, without which there can be no Church of Christ? If the power and authority be, by any possibility, of human origin, there never has been a Church of Christ on earth, and the alleged saving ordinances of the gospel have never been other than empty forms.

23. Our review of the Great Apostasy as presented in this treatise, does not call for any detailed or critical study of the Roman Catholic Church as it exists in modern times, nor of any of the numerous Protestant denominations that have come into existence as dissenting children of the so-called "Mother Church." The apostasy was complete, as far as actual loss of priesthood and cessation of spiritual power in the Church are concerned, long prior to the sixteenth century revolt, known in history as the Reformation. It is instructive to observe, however, that the weakness of the Protestant sects as to any claim to divine appointment

and authority, is recognized by those churches themselves. The Church of England, which, as shown, originated in revolt against the Roman Catholic Church and its pope, is without foundation of claim to divine authority in its priestly orders, unless, indeed, it dare assert the absurdity that kings and parliaments can create and take unto themselves heavenly authority by enactment of earthly statutes.

24. The Roman Catholic Church is at least consistent in its claim that a line of succession in the priesthood has been maintained from the apostolic age to the present, though the claim is utterly untenable in the light of a rational interpretation of history. But the fact remains that the Catholic Church is the only organization venturing to assert the present possession of the holy priesthood by unbroken descent from the apostles of our Lord. The Church of England, chief among the Protestant sects, and all other dissenting churches, are by their own admission and by the circumstances of their origin, man-made institutions, without a semblance of claim to the powers and authority of the holy priesthood.

25. As late as 1896 the question of the validity of the priestly orders in the Church of England was officially and openly discussed and considered, both in England and at Rome. Lord Halifax, chairman of the English Church Union conferred with the Vatican authorities to ascertain the possibility of bringing about closer union between the Roman Catholic Church and the Church of England. This involved the question of the recognition of the priestly orders of the Anglican Church by the pope and Church of Rome. The movement was favored in the interests of unity and peace by the English premier, Mr. Gladstone. The pope, Leo XIII, finally issued a decree refusing to recog-

nize in any degree the authority of the Anglican orders, and expressly declaring all claims to priestly authority by the Church of England as absolutely invalid.

26. Assuredly the Church of Rome could take no other action than this and maintain the consistency of its own claim to exclusive possession of the priesthood by descent. Assuredly the Church of England would have sought no official recognition of its priestly status by the Church of Rome had it any independent claim to the power and authority of the priesthood. The Roman Catholic Church declares that all Protestant denominations are either apostate organizations, or institutions of human creation that have never had even a remote connection with the church that claims succession in the priesthood. In short, the apostate "Mother Church" aggressively proclaims the perfidy of her offspring.

THE APOSTASY ADMITTED.

27. The fact of the great apostasy is admitted. Many theologians who profess a belief in Christianity have declared the fact. Thus we read: "We must not expect to see the Church of Christ existing in its perfection on the earth. It is not to be found thus perfect, either in the collected fragments of Christendom or still less in any one of those fragments."[g]

28. John Wesley, who lived from 1703 to 1791 A. D., and who ranks as chief among the founders of Methodism, comments as follows on the apostasy of the Christian Church as evidenced by the early decline of spiritual power and the cessation of the gifts and graces of the Spirit of God within the Church: "It does not appear that these extraordinary

---

[g]Smith's "Dictionary of the Bible."

gifts of the Holy Spirit[h] were common in the Church for
more than two or three centuries. We seldom hear of them
after that fatal period when the Emperor Constantine called
himself a Christian, and from a vain imagination of pro-
moting the Christian cause thereby heaped riches and power
and honor upon Christians in general, but in particular upon
the Christian clergy. From this time they almost totally
ceased, very few instances of the kind being found. The
cause of this was not, as has been supposed, because there
was no more occasion for them, because all the world was
become Christians. This is a miserable mistake; not a twen-
tieth part of it was then nominally Christians. The real
cause of it was that the love of many, almost all Christians,
so-called, was waxed cold. The Christians had no more of
the spirit of Christ than the other heathens. The Son of Man,
when He came to examine His Church, could hardly find
faith upon earth. This was the real cause why the extraordinary gifts of the Holy Ghost were no longer to be found
in the Christian church—because the Christians were turned
heathens again, and only had a dead form left."[i]

29. The Church of England makes official declaration of
degeneracy and loss of divine authority in these words:
"Laity and clergy, learned and unlearned, all ages, sects,
and degrees, have been drowned in abominable idolatry
most detested by God and damnable to man for eight
hundred years and more."[j] The "Book of Homilies," in which
occurs this declaration by the Church of England, dates
from about the middle of the sixteenth century. According
to this official statement, therefore, the religious world had

[h]See I Cor., ch .12.
[i]John Wesley's Works, Vol. VII, 89: 26-27. See Note 3, end of
chapter.
[j]Church of England "Homily on Perils of Idolatry," p. 3.

been utterly apostate for eight centuries prior to the establishment of the Church of England. The fact of a universal apostasy was widely proclaimed, for the homilies from which the foregoing citation is taken were "appointed to be read in churches" in lieu of sermons under specified conditions. _____

30. *The great apostasy was divinely predicted; its accomplishment is attested by both sacred and secular writ.*

_____

31. To the faithful Latter-day Saint, a concluding proof of the universal apostasy and of the absolute need of a restoration of Priesthood from the heavens will be found in the divine reply to the inquiry of the boy prophet, Joseph Smith, as to which of all the contending sects was right: "I was answered that I must join none of them, for they were all wrong; and the personage who addressed me said that all their creeds were an abomination in his sight; that those professors were all corrupt; that 'they draw near to me with their lips, but their hearts are far from me; they teach for doctrines the commandments of men, having a form of godliness, but they deny the power thereof.' "[k]

THE SEQUEL.

32. The sequel of the Great Apostasy is the Restoration of the Gospel, marking the inauguration of the Dispensation of the Fulness of Times. This epoch-making event occurred in the early part of the nineteenth century, when the Father and the Son manifested themselves to man, and when the Holy Priesthood with all its powers and authority was again brought to earth.

_____

[k]Pearl of Great Price, p. 85, par. 19.

33. The Church of Jesus Christ of Latter-day Saints proclaims to the world this glorious restoration,—at once the consummation of the work of God throughout the ages past, and the final preparation for the second advent of Jesus, the Christ. The Church affirms that after the long night of spiritual darkness, the light of heaven has again come; and that the Church of Christ is authoritatively established. The Church of Jesus Christ of Latter-day Saints stands alone in the declaration that the Holy Priesthood is operative upon earth, not as an inheritance through earthly continuation from the apostolic age, but as the endowment of a new dispensation, brought to earth by heavenly ministration. In this restoration, divinely predicted and divinely achieved, has been witnessed a realization of the Revelator's vision:

"AND I SAW ANOTHER ANGEL FLY IN THE MIDST OF HEAVEN, HAVING THE EVERLASTING GOSPEL TO PREACH UNTO THEM THAT DWELL ON THE EARTH, AND TO EVERY NATION, AND KINDRED, AND TONGUE, AND PEOPLE, SAYING WITH A LOUD VOICE, FEAR GOD AND GIVE GLORY TO HIM; FOR THE HOUR OF HIS JUDGMENT IS COME; AND WORSHIP HIM THAT MADE HEAVEN AND EARTH, AND THE SEA AND THE FOUNTAINS OF WATER."[l]

Notes.

1. PAPIST TESTIMONY TO THE CORRUPTION OF THE CHURCH. "The judicious student of ecclesiastical history will observe that I constantly endeavor to draw my proofs from the most unexceptionable sources. For example: To prove the corrupt state of the clergy, and the abominable practices of the Roman See, I would produce the evidence of George of Saxony, a most bigoted papist, whom the

[l]Rev. 14: 6, 7 For treatment of the Restoration of the Gospel see the Author's "Articles of Faith," Lecture 11. See Notes 4 and 5, end of chapter.

Roman Catholics always reckon among the most sincere and most active of the holy defenders of their religion. Now, as with them the assertions of Luther and the other reformers go for nothing but exaggerations, misrepresentations, or direct falsehoods, let them listen at least to this duke, their steady friend and advocate, who generally, in religious concerns, opposed his relation, the elector of Saxony, and who also entirely approved of Luther's condemnation at Worms. This George of Saxony exhibited to the Diet twelve heads of the grievances which called loudly for reform. Two of these are briefly as follows: 1. Indulgences, which ought to be obtained by prayers, fastings, benevolence towards our neighbor, and other good works, are sold for money. Their value is extolled beyond all decency. The sole object is to gain a deal of money. Hence the preachers, who are bound to set forth truth, teach men nothing but lies and frauds. They are not only suffered to go on thus, but are well paid for their fraudulent harangues. The reason is, the more conviction they can produce among their hearers, the more money flows into the chest. Rivers of scandalous proceedings arise from this corrupt fountain. The officials of the bishops are equally attentive to scrape money together. They vex the poor with their censures for great crimes, as whoredom, adultery, blasphemy; but they spare the rich. The clergy commit the very same crimes, and nobody censures them. Faults which ought to be expiated by prayers and fastings are atoned for by money, in order that the officials may pay large sums to their respective bishops, and retain a portion of the gain for themselves. Neither when a mulct is inflicted, is it done in a way to stop the commission of the same fault in future, but rather so that the delinquent understands he may soon do that very thing again, provided he be but ready to pay. Hence all the sacraments are sold for money; and where that is not to be had, they are absolutely neglected. 2. Another distinct head of the grievances produced by this zealous duke was expressed thus: The scandalous conduct of the clergy is a very fruitful source of the destruction of poor souls. There must be a universal reformation; and this cannot be better effected than by a general council. It is therefore the most earnest wish of us all that such a measure be adopted." (Milner, "Church History," Cent. XVI, ch. 6, footnote.)

2. EXTREMES INCIDENT TO THE REFORMATION. "What were the reproaches constantly applied to the Reformation by its enemies?

Which of its results are thrown in its face, as it were, unanswerable. The two principal reproaches are, first, the multiplicity of sects, the excessive license of thought, the destruction of all spiritual authority, and the entire dissolution of religious society; secondly, tyranny and persecution. 'You provoke licentiousness,' it has been said to the Reformers: 'you produce it; and, after being the cause of it, you wish to restrain and repress it. And how do you repress it? By the most harsh and violent means. You take upon yourselves, too, to punish heresy, and that by virtue of an illegitimate authority.' "—Guizot.

"The Sectarian Dogma of Justification by Faith alone has exercised an influence for evil since the early days of Christianity. The idea upon which this pernicious doctrine was founded, was at first associated with that of an absolute predestination, by which man was foredoomed to destruction, or to an utterly undeserved salvation. Thus, Luther taught as follows: 'The excellent, infallible, and sole preparation for grace, is the eternal election and predestination of God.' 'Since the fall of man, free-will is but an idle word.' 'A man who imagines to arrive at grace by doing all that he is able to do, adds sin to sin, and is doubly guilty.' 'That man is not justified who performs many works; but he who without works has much faith in Christ.' (For these and other doctrines of the Reformation see D'Aubigne's 'History of the Reformation,' Vol. I, pp. 82, 83, 119, 122.) In Milner's 'Church History' (Vol. IV, p. 514) we read: 'The point which the reformer Luther had most at heart in all his labors, contests and dangers, was the justification by faith alone.' Melanchthon voices the doctrine of Luther in these words: 'Man's justification before God proceeds from faith alone. This faith enters man's heart by the grace of God alone;' and further, 'As all things which happen, happen necessarily, according to the divine predestination, there is no such thing as liberty in our wills.' (D' Aubigne, Vol. III, p. 340.) It is true that Luther strongly denounced, and vehemently disclaimed responsibility for, the excesses to which this teaching gave rise, yet he was not less vigorous in proclaiming the doctrine. Note his words: 'I, Doctor Martin Luther, unworthy herald of the doctrine of our Lord Jesus Christ, confess this article, that faith alone without works justifies before God; and I declare that it shall stand and remain forever in despite of the emperor of the Romans, the emperor of the Turks, the emperor of the Persians,—in spite of the pope and all the cardinals, with the bishops, priests, monks and nuns,—in spite

of kings, princes and nobles, and in spite of all the world and of
the devils themselves; and that if they endeavor to fight against this
truth they will draw the fires of hell upon their heads. This is the
true and holy gospel, and the declaration of me, Doctor Luther,
according to the teachings of the Holy Ghost.'" See the Author's
"Articles of Faith," Lecture V, Note 2.

3. DIVERSE VIEWS CONCERNING CONTINUANCE OR DECLINE OF SPIR-
ITUAL GIFTS. "Protestant writers insist that the age of miracles closed
with the fourth or fifth century, and that after that the extraordinary
gifts of the Holy Ghost must not be looked for. Catholic writers, on
the other hand, insist that the power to perform miracles has always
continued in the Church; yet those spiritual manifestations which
they describe after the fourth and fifth centuries savor of invention
on the part of the priests, and childish credulity on the part of the
people; or else, what is claimed to be miraculous falls far short of
the power and dignity of those spiritual manifestations which the
primitive church was wont to witness. The virtues and prodigies,
ascribed to the bones and other relics of the martyrs and saints, are
puerile in comparison with the healings by the anointing with oil
and the laying on of hands, speaking in tongues, interpretations,
prophecies, revelations, casting out of devils in the name of Jesus
Christ; to say nothing of the gifts of faith, wisdom, knowledge,
discernment of spirits, etc.—common in the Church in the days of
the apostles (I Cor. xii, 8-10). Nor is there anything in the scriptures or in reason that would lead one to believe that they were to
be discontinued. Still this plea is made by modern Christians—ex-
plaining the absence of these spiritual powers among them—that the
extraordinary gifts of the Holy Ghost were only intended to accom-
pany the proclamation of the gospel during the first few centuries, until the church was able to make its way without them, and they
were to be done away. It is sufficient to remark upon this that it is
assumption pure and simple, and stands without warrant either of
scripture or right reason; and proves that men had so far changed
the religion of Jesus Christ that it became a form of godliness without the power thereof." (B. H. Roberts, "Outlines of Ecclesiastical
History, " Part II, Sec. V. 6-8.)

4. COMMENTARY ON THE REVELATOR'S VISION OF THE RESTORA-
TION. It is instructive to inquire into the interpretation given by bib-

lical students to the prophecy voiced by John the Revelator predicting the advent of the angel "having the everlasting gospel." Dr.
Clarke offers the following reflections on the passage: *"And I saw
another angel fly in the midst of heaven, having the everlasting
gospel*: Whether this angel means any more than a particular dispensation of providence and grace, by which the gospel shall be rapidly
sent throughout the whole world; or whether it mean any especial
messenger, order of preachers, people, or society of Christians, whose
professed object it is to send the gospel of the kingdom throughout
the earth, we know not. But the vision seems truly descriptive of a
late institution, entitled "The British and Foreign Bible Society,"
whose object it is to print and circulate the scriptures of the Old and
New Testaments through all the habitable world, and in all the
languages spoken on the face of the earth" (Clarke, "Bible Commentary," Rev. 14: 6.)

The learned commentator is to be commended for his frank avowal
as to uncertainty regarding the precise interpretation of this scripture, and for the provisional and tentative manner in which he indi-
cates a possible application to the wide distribution of the Holy Bible
through the efforts of a most worthy and influential society. It is to
be noted that Dr. Clarke wrote his famous commentary on the Bible
shortly before the actual restoration of the gospel through angelic
agency which resulted in the establishment of the Church of Jesus
Christ of Latter-day Saints. Of necessity his search for the fulfilment
of the prediction was unsatisfactory, and, indeed, unsuccessful, inasmuch as the fulfilment had not then occurred. The commendable
work of the Bible Society was a preparation for the fulfilment of the
momentous prophecy, but not the fulfilment itself.

5. RESTORATION OF THE CHURCH. "In the first ten centuries immediately following the ministry of Christ, the authority of the priesthood was lost from among men, and no human power could restore
it. But the Lord in His mercy provided for the re-establishment of
His Church in the last days, and for the last time; and prophets of
olden time foresaw this era of renewed enlightenment, and sang in
joyous tones of its coming." (See Dan. 2: 44, 45; 7: 27; Matt. 24: 14;
Rev. 14: 6-8.) "This restoration was effected by the Lord through
the prophet, Joseph Smith, who, together with Oliver Cowdery, in
1829, received the Aaronic Priesthood under the hands of John the

Baptist, and later the Melchizedek Priesthood under the hands of the former-day apostles, Peter, James, and John. By the authority thus bestowed, the Church has been again organized with all its former completeness, and mankind once more rejoices in the priceless privilege of the counsels of God. The Latter-day Saints declare their high claim to the true Church organization, similar in all essentials to the organization effected by Christ among the Jews; these people of the last days profess to have the Priesthood of the Almighty, the power to act in the name of God, which power commands respect both on earth and in heaven." (The Author, "Articles of Faith," Lecture 11: 12.)

INDEX

mony as to corruption in the Church, 164.

Gibbon, Edward, cited as to imprudent enthusiasm of early Christians, 83, 91; as to "libels," 84; as to number of persecutions by Romans, 77; as to cause of pagan opposition to Christianity, 76; as to Church dissensions during peace, 92; as to heathen mysteries in the early Church, 109; as to Church ceremonial during fifth century, 124.

Gnostics, 98, 109.

God, foreknowledge of, 19.

Gospel, contrasted with the Law, 3; preached extensively in apostolic age, 9; restored, 163, 169.

Greek and Roman Catholics, 133.

Gregory, Thaumaturgus, 123.

Guizot, cited as to extremes incident to the Reformation, 166.

Heathen innovations in the early Church, 113.

Hegesippus, cited as to early apostasy, 45.

Helaman instructed by Alma as to the apostasy, 32.

Henry VIII of England, establishment of Church of England by, 157.

Heresies and schisms in the early Church, 93.

Herodians, 3.

Homily of Church of England, on idolatry, 162.

"Host," adoration of the, 121.

Huss, John, 151.

Images, adoration of, 115.

Indians, North American, 17, 33.

Indulgences, 137; sale of 134; Roman Church responsible for the practice, 142.

Infant baptism, a heresy, 119; historical notes on, 126.

Iniquity, mystery of; commentary on, 42.

Inordinate zeal by early Christians, 91.

Inquisition, the, 154.

Internal causes of the apostasy, 82.

Internal dissensions in Church during times of peace, 92.

Jerome of Prague, 151.

Jerusalem, destruction of, by Romans, 63.

Jews, condition of, at time of Christ's birth, 1; distinguished from pagans, 2; early persecution of Church by, 62.

John, the Revelator, predictions of the apostasy by, 30; his messages to the churches in Asia, 44; commentary on his vision of the Restoration, 168.

Judaism, 57; admixture of, with Christianity, 97.

Judaistic persecution of the Church, 57.

Jude, his prediction of the apostasy, 30; his testimony as to early apostasy, 43, 52.

Lamanites, origin of, 11, 16.

Latter-day Saints, Church of Jesus Christ of, 33, 163, 169.

Law of Moses, 3; distinct from "the everlasting covenant," 25.

"Libels" in early Church history, 84.

Limborch, cited on infant baptism, 127.

Logos, the, 101.

Lord's Supper, changes in administration of, 119.

Luther, Martin, his attack on certain practices of the Roman Church, 152; brings about the Reformation, 152; his declaration at Diet of Worms, 153; his death, 153; cited on infant

174 INDEX.

baptism, 127; on justification
by faith, 166.

MacKnight, cited as to the apos-
tate church, 149.
Marcus Aurelius, persecution un-
der, 71.
Martyr, Justin, cited as to early
form of baptism, 125.
Martyr worship, inception of, 83.
Martyrdom, early devotion to, 82.
Matthias, one of the twelve apos-
tles, 7.

Melanchthon, Philip, 153.

Metropolitans, origin of title, 132.

Milner, Joseph, 52; cited as to
evils in the early Church, 86;
as to early decline of Church,
94; as to condition of the
Church in third century, 86;
as to early evidences of apostasy, 90; as to perversion of
the sacrament, 121; as to condition of the Church at close
of first century, 47.

Monks and monasteries, 105.

Mormon, Book of; citations from,
as to establishment of Church
on western hemisphere, 10; as
to origin of Nephites and Lamanites, 16; as to predictions
of apostasy on western hemisphere, 32; as to growth of
apostasy on western hemi-
sphere, 48.

Moroni, the last Nephite scribe,
49.

Moses, Law of, 3; not "the everlasting covenant," 25.

Mosheim, J. L., 52; cited as to
paganism at beginning of
Christian era, 14; as to divine
aid in apostolic ministry, 15,
as to early schisms in Church,
46; as to number of Roman
persecutions, 77; as to perversion of the sacrament, 121; as

to extent of Neronian persecution, 78; as to early declension of Church, 94, 95; as to
heathen innovations in Church,
113; as to transubstantiation,
120; as to early church organization, 131.
"Mother Church," the, 161.
Myers, P. V. N., cited as to
cause of pagan persecution of
Church, 72; as to conditions
at close of fifteenth century,
151; as to the Inquisition, 155.
Mysteries, heathen, imitation of,
in the Church, 109.
"Mystery of iniquity," comments
on, 42, 50.

Neander, Johann, cited as to in-
fant baptism, 126.
Nephi, his prediction of apostasy
on western hemisphere, 33.
Nephites, origin of, 11, 16; de-
struction of, 49.
Nero, persecution under, 68, 78.
New Platonics, 100.
Newton, Bishop, cited as to the
apostate church, 148.
Nice, Council of, 102.
Nicene Creed, 103.
Nicolaitanes, perfidy of, 97, 107.
Number of persecutions of Chris-
tians by Romans, 67, 77.

Paganism at beginning of Christian era, 14.
Pagans distinguished from Jews,
2; persecution of Christians by,
64; opposition of, explained, 76;
they affiliate with the Church,
113.
Papacy, history of, 140, 144.
Papist testimony to corruption in
the Church, 164.
Paul, Apostle, his predictions of
the apostasy, 28; his testimony
to early beginning of the apostasy, 40.